BROTHER TO DRAGONS

Robert Penn Warren

BROTHER
TO
DRAGONS

A Tale in Verse and Voices

A NEW VERSION

Random House
New York

Library of Congress Cataloging in Publication Data

Warren, Robert Penn, 1905–
Brother to dragons.

1. Jefferson, Thomas, Pres. U. S., 1743–1826—Poetry.
2. Lewis, Lucy Jefferson, 1752–1811—Poetry.
3. Lewis, Isham, d. 1815?—Poetry. 4. Lewis, Lilburn,
d. 1812—Poetry. I. Title.
PS3545.A748B7 1979   811'.5'2   79–10782
ISBN 0-394-50551-4

Manufactured in the United States of America

2 4 6 8 9 7 5 3

First Edition

To Cleanth and Tinkum Brooks

An old Indian expressed to Col. Moore great astonishment that white people could live in a country which had been the scene of such conflicts. An old Sac warrior, whom Col. Joseph Hamilton Daviess met in St. Louis in 1800, gave utterance to similar expressions of surprise. Kentucky he said was filled with the ghosts of its slaughtered inhabitants: how could the white man make it his home?

HISTORY OF CHRISTIAN COUNTY, by W. H. Perrin
(Chicago and Louisville, 1884)

. . . when it shake the earth don't be afraid no harm anybody

Letter of Wovoka, the Messiah—Arapaho version
FOURTEENTH ANNUAL REPORT OF THE BUREAU OF
ETHNOLOGY, Part 2 (Washington, 1893)

For as children tremble and fear everything in the blind darkness, so we in the light sometimes fear what is no more to be feared than the things that children in the dark hold in terror and imagine will come true. This terror, therefore, and darkness of the mind must be dispersed, not by the rays of the sun nor the bright shaft of daylight, but by the aspect and law of nature.

Lucretius: DE RERUM NATURA, III
(translated by W. H. D. Rouse)

FOREWORD

In the fall of 1807 Colonel* Charles Lewis, an aristocratic planter of
Albemarle County, Virginia, removed to western Kentucky and settled
himself not far from the frontier village of Smithland, in Livingston
County, upriver from Paducah near the confluence of the Ohio and Cumberland rivers. This was, in fact, a family migration. The plan seems to
have been developed by and dependent upon two of the Lewis sons,
Randolph, who bought (for $9,100) 3,833⅓ acres on the Ohio, and
Lilburne, who bought (for $8,000) 1,500 acres, somewhat lower down-
river, but still well above Paducah, both tracts largely undeveloped.
Colonel Lewis and Lucy (he had married the sister of Thomas Jefferson), once rich but now on evil days, spent time sporadically on the new
family holdings, as did Isham, a younger son, something of a feckless
wanderer with no fixed occupation. And there were, of course, a number
of slaves (though not enough for the task of adequately clearing land),
among them a teen-age boy named George (John in my version), a
sort of body-servant and handyman for Lilburne.

On a bluff overlooking the Ohio, Lilburne built his house, "Rocky
Hill," presumably rather grand for time and place, with quarters and
other outbuildings. After the death of Lucy, who was buried on
Randolph's land, Colonel Lewis seems to have spent less and less time at
"Rocky Hill." About the same time Lilburne's first wife died, but he
married again, this time to Letitia, a daughter of one of the local families,
Rutter by name. This wife was at "Rocky Hill," pregnant in 1811, when
George met his tragic end.

I have stayed within the general outline of the available record, but
have altered certain details. In my version Lilburne's first wife does not
appear, and I have disposed of a raft of young children as irrelevant to
my theme. I omit the presence of Colonel Lewis† in Kentucky in May,
1812, before the trial of Isham. I have placed Lucy's grave at "Rocky

* Sometimes said to have been a physician.
† Colonel Lewis appears at the proving of Lilburne's will at the May session of the
County Court of that year.

xi

Hill," substituting it for that of Lilburne's first wife—this for thematic reasons. I have filled in certain gaps in narrative, motivation, and theme. For instance, I have invented a story for Letitia and her husband, and have invented two characters: Aunt Cat, from whole cloth; and the brother of Letitia, who has only a shadowy existence in the record.

My poem, in fact, had its earliest suggestion in bits of folk tale, garbled accounts heard in my boyhood. Then came a reference or two, years later, in print. Then, as the poem began to take shape in my head, I went to Smithland and sought out in the dim and dusty hugger-mugger of a sort of half-basement room (as I remember it) the little bundles of court records, suffering from damp and neglect, but some-times tied up in faded red tape or string.

My first version of *Brother to Dragons*, the poem, was published in 1953. Only in 1977 appeared a conscientious and scholarly account of the general subject, from Virginia days and genealogies forward, *Jefferson's Nephews*, by Boynton Merrill, Jr. (now the owner of much of the Lewis estate). This book, fascinating and reliable as it is, does not change the basic thematic or dramatic outline of my tale. For in-stance, though Colonel Lewis takes refuge in Kentucky after his financial difficulties, this practical failure, though solving an old mystery, does not necessarily displace the sense of inner failure from which the Colonel suffers in the poem—and which might meld with the sense of more practical failure. It must have been hard to invite daily comparison for years with a brother-in-law of the stature of Jefferson, who, it would seem, had no great concern for him in the first place, and whom he, in the end, defrauded—this according to Merrill's account.

In regard to the role of Jefferson, nothing is changed. Although the tragedy in Kentucky was published in the press at the time, several eminent students of his life and work assured me, when I was working on the first version, that they could find no reference by him to the Kentucky story, and one scholar even went so far as to state in a letter his feeling that Jefferson could not bring himself to discuss—or perhaps even to face—the appalling episode. If this is true (though the chances of further research may make it untrue), it is convenient for my poem; but the role of Jefferson in the poem, or in history, does not stand or fall by the fact. If the moral shock to Jefferson administered by the discovery of what was possible in his blood should turn out to be some-what literally short of what is here represented, subsequent events in the history of our nation, which he helped to found, might amply supply the defect.

xii

The story of Meriwether Lewis, the cousin of Lilburne and Isham Lewis, and a kinsman of Jefferson himself, to whom he served as a secretary and to whom he stood in a sort of filial relation, is, as far as my poem is concerned, drawn from the journals of the Lewis and Clark expedition. Both Lilburne and Meriwether Lewis entered the wilderness as heralds of civilization, as "light-bringers," and my story is about the difference with which they performed the role and their tragic ends, Meriwether's apparently by suicide. Jefferson wrote a biography of poor Meriwether. There is some evidence, which does not strike me as necessarily convincing, that Meriwether was murdered. But certainly there was in the Lewis blood a strain of what Jefferson referred to as "hypochondriacal affection," as is well evidenced by Lilburne. In any case, Jefferson believed that the death was by suicide committed in despair at the injustice of the charges brought against him as Governor of the Louisiana Territory.

I know that any discussion of the relation of this poem to its historical materials is, in one perspective, irrelevant to its value; and it could be totally accurate as history and still not worth a dime as a poem. I am trying to write a poem, not a history, and therefore have no compunction about tampering with non-essential facts. But poetry is more than fantasy and is committed to the obligation of trying to say something, however obliquely, about the human condition. Therefore, a poem dealing with history is no more at liberty to violate what the writer takes to be the spirit of his history than it is at liberty to violate what he takes to be the nature of the human heart. What he takes those things to be is, of course, his ultimate gamble.

This is another way of saying that I have tried in my poem to make, in a thematic way, historical sense along with whatever kind of sense it may otherwise be happy enough to make.

Historical sense and poetic sense should not, in the end, be contradictory, for if poetry is the little myth we make, history is the big myth we live, and in our living, constantly remake.

As I have said, the first version of this poem appeared in 1953, and has run through a number of printings. It may, no doubt, seem odd that at this late date another and very different version should be issued. But this new version is the work, sometimes very sporadic, of some twenty years, and is, in some important senses, a new work. There had been, to begin with, some confusion about the text printed. But as I began to live with the text, sometimes in an off-and-on process of preparation for the stage,* my dissatisfaction with several features grew. Now there are a number of cuts made from the original version, and some additions. Meriwether is given a more significant role. There is, in large measure, a significant change of rhythm. A number of dramatic effects are sharpened. Though the basic action and theme remain the same, there is, I trust, an important difference in the total "feel." For the reworking was not merely a slow and patchwork job. It meant, before the end, a protracted and concentrated reliving of the whole process.

* A dramatic version was optioned for Broadway in the middle 1950's, and after months of work on text and casting, blew up on signing day. A later version was produced by the American Place Theater in New York, in 1964, and under the direction of Adrian Hall, at the Trinity Theater of Providence, several runs occurred, most recently a tour, with the text and production considerably revised, ending in the Wilbur Theater, in Boston.

I have spoken of stage versions drawn from this poem. But even if the present version is a dialogue spoken by characters, it is definitely not a play, and must not be taken as such. The main body of the action lies in the remote past—in the earthly past of characters long dead—and now they meet at an unspecified place and unspecified time and try to make sense of the action in which they were involved. We may take them to appear and disappear as their urgencies of argument swell and subside. The place of this meeting is, we may say, "no place," and the time is "any time." This is but a way of saying that the issues that the characters here discuss are, in my view at least, a human constant.

BROTHER TO DRAGONS

THOMAS JEFFERSON: *The third President of the United States, who bought the Great West from Napoleon, but, in some ultimate vanity, neglected to mention that fact, or the fact that he had been President, when he composed the triple boast for his epitaph. The epitaph is now carved on his monument on the mountain where Monticello stands, in Albemarle County, Virginia:*

> *Author*
> *Of The Declaration of*
> *American Independence*
> *Of*
> *The Statute Of Virginia*
> *For Religious Freedom, And*
> *Father Of The University*
> *Of Virginia*

R.P.W.: *The writer of this poem*

MERIWETHER LEWIS: *A kinsman of Thomas Jefferson, and at one time secretary to him. With Clark, the commander of the expedition to open the Louisiana Territory and define the road to the Pacific. Upon his return, the Governor of the Territory*

COLONEL CHARLES LEWIS: *Husband of Lucy Jefferson, the sister of the President*

LUCY JEFFERSON LEWIS: *Sister of Thomas Jefferson*

LILBURNE LEWIS: *Son of Charles and Lucy Lewis*

LETITIA LEWIS: *Wife to Lilburne Lewis*

AUNT CAT: *A slave in the household of Charles Lewis, and black Mammy to Lilburne*

BROTHER: *To Letitia Lewis*

ISHAM LEWIS: *Youngest son of Charles and Lucy Lewis, brother to Lilburne*

JOHN: *A young slave*

PLACE: *No place*   TIME: *Any time*

* This symbol is used to indicate a space between sections of a poem wherever such spaces are lost in pagination.

I

My name is Jefferson. Thomas. I
Lived. Died. But
Dead, cannot lie down in the
Dark. Cannot, though dead, set
My mouth to the dark stream that I may unknow
All my knowing. Cannot, for if,
Kneeling in that final thirst, I thrust
Down my face, I see come glimmering upward,
White, white out of the absolute dark of depth,
My face. And it is only human.

Have you ever tried to kiss that face in the mirror?
Or—ha, ha—has it ever tried to kiss you? Well,
You are only human. Is that a boast?

R.P.W.: Well, I've read your boast
Cut in stone, on the mountain, off in Virginia.

JEFFERSON: What else had I in age to cling to,
Even in the face of knowledge?
I tried to bring myself to say:
Knowledge is only incidental, hope is all—
Hope, a dry acorn, but some green germ
May split it yet, then joy and the summer shade.
Even after age and the tangle of experience
I still might—
Oh, grandeur green and murmuring instancy of leaf,
Beneath that shade we'll shelter. So, in senility
And moments of indulgent fiction I might try
To defend my old definition of man.

In Philadelphia first it came, my heart
Shook, shamefast in glory, and I saw, I saw—
But I'll tell you quietly, in system, what I saw.
In Philadelphia—delegates by accident, in essence men,

Marmosets in mantles, beasts in boots, parrots in pantaloons,
That is to say, men. Only ourselves, in the end,
Offal of history, tangents of our father's pitiful lust
At midnight heat or dawn-bed ease of a Sunday.
Why should that fuddling glory,
The gasp and twitch of our begetting, seem
Pitiful? Is it not worthy of us?
Or we of it? Too much crowds in
To break the thread of discourse and make me forget
That irony is always, and only, a trick of light on the late landscape.

But what I had meant to say, we were only ourselves,
Packed with our personal lusts and languors, lost,
Every man-jack of us, in some blind alley, enclave,
Crank cul-de-sac, couloir, or corridor
Of Time. Or Self.
And in that dark, no thread,
Airy as breath by an Ariadne's fingers forged—
No thread, and beyond some groped-at corner, hulked
In the dark, hock-deep in ordure, its beard
And shag foul-scabbed, and when the hoof heaves—
Listen!—the foulness sucks like mire.

He waits. He is the infamy of Crete.
He is the midnight's enormity. And is
Our brother, our darling brother. And Pasiphaë!
Dear mother, mother of all, poor Pasiphaë—
Huddled and hutched in the cow's hide,
Laced, latched, thonged up, and breathlessly ass-humped
For the ecstatic stroke.

What was your silence then?

Before the scream?

And through the pain, like a curtain split,
In your mind did you see some meadow green,
Some childhood haven, water and birdsong, and you a child?

The bull plunged. You screamed like a girl, and strove.

6

But the infatuate machine of your invention held.
Later they lifted you out and wiped
Foam from your lips in the dark palace.

We have not loved you less, poor Pasiphaë.

Even if, after all, it was your own invention.

But no, God no!—I tell you my mother's name was **Jane**.
She was Jane Randolph, born in England,
Baptized in the Parish of Shadwell, London.

Yes, what was I saying? Language betrays.
There are no words to tell Truth.

To begin again. When I to Philadelphia came
I knew what the world was. Oh, I wasn't
That ilk of a fool! Then when I saw individual evil,
I rationally said, it is only provisional paradox
To resolve itself in Time. Oh, easy,
Plump-bellied comfort!

Philadelphia, yes. I knew we were only men,
Defined in our errors and interests. But I, a man too—
Yes, laugh if you will—stumbled into
The breathless awe of vision, saw sudden
On every face, face after face,
Bleared, puffed, lank, lean red-fleshed or sallow, all—
On all saw the brightness blaze,
And knew my own days,
Times, hopes, horsemanship, respect of peers,
Delight, desire, and even my love, but straw
Fit for the flame, and in that fierce combustion, I—
Why, I was nothing, nothing but joy,
And my heart cried out:
"Oh, this is Man!"

And thus my minotaur. There at the blind
Labyrinthine turn of my personal time—

7

What do they call it? Yes,
Nel mezzo del cammin—yes, then met
The beast, in beauty masked. And the time
I met it was—at least, it seems so now—
That moment when the first alacrity
Of blood stumbles, and all natural joy
Sees Nature but as a mirror for its natural doom.
And so to hold joy you must deny mere Nature, and leap
Beyond man's natural bourne and constriction
To find justification in a goal
Hypothesized in Nature.

Well, thus the infatuate encounter. But
No beast then, the towering
Definition, angelic, arrogant, abstract,
Greaved in glory, thewed with light, the bright
Brow tall as dawn.

I could not see the eyes.

So seized the pen, and in the upper room,
With the excited consciousness that I was somehow
Rectified, annealed, my past annulled
And fate confirmed, wrote. And far off,
In darkness, the watch called out.

Time came, we signed the document, went home.
I had not seen the eyes of that bright apparition.
I had been blind with light.

I did not know its eyes were blind.

The fat was in the fire.
And I who once said, all liberty
Is bought with blood, must now say,
All truth is bought with blood, and the blood is ours,
But only the truth can make us free—
Free from the fool lie.
And doom is always domestic, it purrs like a cat,
And the absolute traitor lurks in some sweet corner of the blood.

8

Therefore I walk and wake, and cannot die.
But I will tell you—

There was a house—

R.P.W.: Yes, I have seen it. Or saw,
Rather, all that remained when time and fire
Had long since done their kindness, and the crime
Could nestle, smug and snug, in any
Comfortable conscience, such as mine—or the next man's—
And over the black stones the rain
Has fallen, falls, with the benign indifferency
Of the historical imagination, while grass,
In idiot innocence, has fingered all to peace.
Anyway, I saw the house—

JEFFERSON: I never saw it. Never crossed
The mountains to Kentucky and my West.
But sent my Meriwether there,
Across the plains, past the last snow-peak to—

MERIWETHER: Sent me—and my heart swelled to go!

JEFFERSON: My cousin, my near-son—oh, son, for I
Had none, and saw you as the level-eyed
And straight-browed ones to come.
I said I cannot go,
But my own blood will go
To name and chart and set the human foot.

MERIWETHER: Oh, yes, I knew that dream. Learned it of you,
And under mountain stars remembered your handgrip
On each of my two shoulders,
Old and bony the grip,
But burned like fire—and then—
Ah, then—the only, first and last, unique
Kiss. You from your towering greatness leaned
To place it on my cheek. And I—

JEFFERSON: 'Twas then I gave name to the

9

Long-felt reality. I called you son. I said:
"The world trusts you, my son. Farewell."

MERIWETHER: I saluted, but
Your face—it was suddenly turned away.

JEFFERSON: Beyond affection and farewell glaze of tears, I saw
My West—the land I bought and gave and never
Saw, but like the Israelite,
From some high pass or crazy crag of mind, saw—
Saw all,
Swale and savannah and the tulip tree
Immortally blossoming to May,
Hawthorn and haw
Valleys extended, prairies idle, and the land's
Long westward languor lifting
Toward the flaming escarpment of the end of day—

MERIWETHER: Saw the sad bison lick the outstretched hand,
And on the western rocks, wracked in wild clang and smother,
The black seal barks and loves us, knowing we will come.

JEFFERSON: It was great Canaan's grander counterfeit.
Bold Louisiana,
The landfall of my soul—
Or then it seemed—

R.P.W.: But—

JEFFERSON: The house—

CHARLES: I built it, and I know
That some, perhaps you too,
Take it and all that therein came to pass
As mark of hid madness and black spleen
I from my fathers took, and in turn
Stuck in the womb of Lucy Jefferson
That she might conceive—and the child's first cry
Was honey in my heart—oh, long ago!
          *

But was I the vessel, vase, and propagator
Of madness? Or was it she?
In any case, I'll say
That madness is but the cancer of truth, the arrogance
Of truth gone wild and swollen in the blood.

Madness is what the sane man wakes to.

I built the house,
Left Albemarle and ease,
Took wife and sons, slaves, chattels, beasts, and goods,
My marks of rank and occupation, all
Those things, intangible and tangible, that men
Clutch round them like a cloak against the time
When wind sits sudden in the dire
Airt, and cold creeps.
I took those things, for they are like
The shell the shellfish spins from the slick slime
And deliquescence of itself to fend
That self, and its poor palpitation, boxed in dark.

Shellfish and man, the same. I, too. I took
Myself and mine,
Mine being myself,
And fled.

Fled—that's the word. Fled the intolerableness
Of a world that I had made. And had made me.
That world and I—
Two mirrors set forever and precisely face to face
To match but gaze for deeper gaze, and so compound
Failure forever inward, each to each.

So fled,
Sought new world, new birth, tension and test, perhaps terror.
Said I'd renew, if for an instant only,
The dear illusion, lost in youth, of being
Some part of human effort, and man's hope.
Said I'd redeem the wild land, set blossom by the stone.
                *

But knew it was illusion. Knew that I fled,
Not as redeemer but the damned.

Ah, better, better, had I singly fled,
Alone and Ishmael where the desert howled
Or trees hid the savage's obscenity,
To hug the foulness of uncivil men—
That had been honest, but instead I built
The house to hide the lie I lived, and was,
And all the trinkets of my emptiness.

R.P.W.: And it is gone.

JEFFERSON: It is not gone, for I, who never saw it,
See it now, and in the unspooling dark
Hear timbers creak and the stair, untrodden, groan.
The earth itself may groan for man's foot,
And therefore am glad my foot is weightless now, **even though knowing**
That the impalpable is not the innocent,
For the house is gone and is not gone, and yet—

R.P.W.: I assure you it is gone. I know the place.
Up Highway 109 from Hopkinsville
To Dawson Springs, then west on 62,
Across Kentucky at the narrow neck.
We ripped the July dazzle on the slab—
July of '46—ripped through the sun-bit land:
Blunt hills eroded red, stunt-oak, scrag-plum,
The ruined coal-tipple and the blistered town,
And farther on, from shade of a shack flung down
Amid sage-grass by the sun-blasted field
A face fixed at us and the red eye glared
Without forgiveness, and will not forgive.

But touch the accelerator and quick you're gone
Beyond forgiveness, pity, hope, hate, love.
So we ripped on, but later when the road
Was empty, stopped just once to void the bladder,
And in that stunning silence after the tire's song
The July-fly screamed like a nerve gone wild.

And then a million
Took up the job, and in that simultaneous outrage
Sunlight screamed, while urine pattered the parched soil.

Above Paducah, east some fifteen miles,
Upriver there, they call it Smithland.
The town, I mean. It never came to much,
Sure not the vainglory the man
Named Smith—whoever the hell he was—had
In mind that morning when they laid the log,
Squared sill, mixed clay for chink, and split the shakes
For the first cabin, back in the seventeen-nineties.
He had a right to hope, that fellow Smith,
In that heyday of hope and the westward heart's extravagance,
When *Grab* was watchword and earth spread her legs
Wide as she could, like any jolly trollop
Back in the bushes after
The preaching or the husking bee, and teased:
"Come git it, boy, hit's yourn, but git it deep."

And every dawn sang "Glory!"
Sang "Glory be to *Grab*, come git it, boy!"
Sang "Boy, hit's yourn, but git it deep!"

Smith had a right, all right; for the town-site
Was noble where the Cumberland discovers
The sober magnificence of the Ohio, and into that sweep pours
All its own wash and wastage up from Tennessee,
And the bluff was noble, and the beech it bore
To guard that stately confluence where
The traffic yawed on westward, like a tide:
Broadhorn and keelboat and the boatman's hail
That shook the shallows while the fiddle skirled—
Half-horse, half-alligator, prodigal
Of blood, sweat, semen, and the God-damn world.
Haired hand on the sweep, and the haired lip lifts for song,
And even the leathery heart foreknows the end and knows
It will not be long, be long,
For a journey is only a journey and only Time is long,

And a river is only water, Time only will always flow:

> *All the way to Shawneetown,*
> *Long time ago.*

That was the song the bull-necked boatman sang
While sunlight shivered and the green bluffs rang
All the way to Shawneetown, long time ago.

The last keel passes, night draws on.
The hickory leaf hangs limp, tomorrow weather.
Past spit and bluffhead now the last note fades
Into the ambiguous opacities of history.
Past chute and snag, broadhorn and brawler gone,
They pass in music: *long time ago*.
They passed in music.
Smithland stays and sleeps.

Long time ago: and never came to much,
For Louisville up the river had the falls
And had the Blue Grass, too, to back it up.
And Smithland nothing, canebrake and gray clay,
And hoot owls aren't a poultry highly prized,
And even now no locomotive scares those owls.
A hundred years behind schedule in '46,
Barring the Dixie Theater and gas pump,
It looked the sort of town Sam Clemens might
Grow up in then and not be much worse off.
River and catfish, nigger in the shade,
Little brick jail your fist could punch a hole in,
But the town bum's too comfortable to care,
It's good as home, or nigh, and his Baby Girl
Comes brings him hoecake like he likes it, hot,
And under the maples, from the courthouse pump,
Draws Pap fresh water. She is eight years old.

But this would not deny there's more in Smithland:
The pillow bitten in the midnight pain
Of love disprized or lust exacerbated,
Ambition burked and the ego oozing like
The secret sore and the suppuration smells.
Here Time contracts on the most sanguine heart,

And malice and stratagem canker in dreams
Like milk gone sour in July.
Yes, people live here even now, and even
The picturesque bum, sudden-awake
In the vomit-sodden dawn,
Cries out the classic anguish of our doom:
"Ain't nobody loves me, I never had no chance!"

And Baby Girl will hate him soon. Why not?

But even so, the town looked still
The sort of town that the vagrant liar from Ithaca
Might have spoken of as of his own rocky sea-mark:
"Not much of a place—but good for raising boys."
Not rock and olive, no, nor dazzling depths
Whence once Poseidon, rearing
From crystal courts and tangled corridors
Of glaucous pearl and ink-slick basalt, stared
Beyond black sea-wrack on the emerald
Of water, white-stung, surf-brilliant, to meet
The sun, and shake
His locks, foam-maned, against the dawn.

No, nothing like that in my own Todd County even—
But when you are twelve a river will serve,
And there's no town
Without some country, and a ruined mill
And millpond, wood-lot, or a fox's den
Is something—or one wild goose that came one fall,
Lost from its constellation that bestrode,
Star-triumphing, the icy altitudes,
While the hoots moved south.
Lost, sick, or old, it settled on a stock-pond,
And heard the imperial clamor darkling fade,
And slept.

'Twas Kent—the boy who shot it just at dawn, threw down his gun,
Crashed the skim-ice, and seized it, hugged it, ran
Three miles to town and yelled for joy and every
Step cried like a baby and did not know why.

Then at the barbershop the hangers-on
Admired the trophy, silent till one said:
"From Canady, come all that way, well I be durn."

Even without the goose, you might have found
The images you'll need when you reach forty
And have to learn the single lesson left
To learn worth learning after
You've laid the BB down for the twelve-gauge,
And that lesson is that the only thing
In life is glory. That's a hard
Thing to learn, and a hard fact to face,
For it knocks society's values to a cocked hat,
Or seems to, for the one thing that man fears
Is the terror of salvation and the face
Of glory. But that face is all. Yes,
Like it or lump it, try to recognize
It in the world's face when, however rarely,
It comes. Oh, remember
Now your seeding and the world's magnificence
To which your heart must answer if it can,
And if you can't, you'd better
Set your affairs in order and sit down
To the careful cultivation of cirrhosis,
For drink's a kind of glory, too, though sleazy, and man
Can't live without some glory after all,
Even a poor kind.

And Smithland too,
Though it never came to much, had citizens
Who for a century and a half were cramming their courthouse
With records of the things they lived by, if not for.
Debris of the local courts, Circuit and County,
In the fusty vaults, blind:
Land transfers, grants, indictments, inquests, plaints,
Stompings and stabbings, public blasphemy,
Lawings and mayhem, the slapdash
Confusions of life flung
In a heap like the kitchen-midden
Of a lost clan feasting while their single fire

Flared red and green with sea-salt, and night fell—
Shellfish and artifact, blacked bone and shard,
Left on the sea-tongued shore,
And the sea was Time.

Just out of Smithland on the Louisville road
You'll find the monument, a simple shaft
The local D.A.R.'s put up in '24
Amid the ragweed, dog-fennel, and cockleburr,
To honor Lucy Lewis for good taste
In dying in Kentucky. The stone
Does name her sister to the President,
But quite neglects her chiefest fame, that she
Gave suck to two black-hearted murderers.
But to return to Lucy, little's known—

LUCY: There is little to know, for I know only
The way the sunlight fell across a leaf in Albemarle.
So long ago in Albemarle. I know only
The tug of lip on nipple and how that small contraction
Made all my being hush to the deep depth
Like water windless under a moon of joy.

I loved my children. Love them. But know, too,
The way my husband's face looked locked in sleep,
When leaning in the night, the lamp unlit,
I said, "He lives in some dark place where I
May come to take his hand, if I love well."
But never came where he inhabited.

Came only to Kentucky, by my love.
I did the best I could. No, that's a lie.
I did not do my best. I died. I know
That if you love enough, no death
Can come to kill you while there's need of you.

Yes, if I had lived,
My love somehow might have sustained my son.
It might have been to him like a hand stretched out.
And Little Isham—oh, Ishey—love might

Have at least been some light against the ignorant torpor
That breathed from the dark land. Yes,
If I had loved,
Loved well enough to live, the tiptoe horror
Had not come sly, to insinuate
Itself in my name to Lilburne, my son.

I saw the dark land creep into my house.
I saw the dark night creep into my bed.
I saw the river-dark swim in my cup.
The screech owl laughed and told me I was dead,
And I believed him, and so I was dead,
But cannot die, nor cease to know
That the human curse is simply to love and sometimes to love well,

But never well enough. It's simple as that.

R.P.W.: There's nothing of that on your monument,
But I know your name means, etymologically, *light*.
There was some need of light in that dark house.

LILBURNE: They put it out, they put
It out—and then—

JEFFERSON: Look! that's the one,
The bloody brother and with his hands—

LUCY: Oh, Lilburne, oh, my son!

LILBURNE: —and then, it was dark.
Listen,
Do you remember when you lay and there was a light,
But just one light, one candle-flame, and all
The world was dark, and the dark sniffed under the door?
Then the gust, cold,
And the flame snapped. It snapped
Like a louse under the wind's thumb,
And dark—

LUCY: Oh, son, forgive me and let me die!

JEFFERSON: There's no forgiveness for our being human.
It is the inexpungable error. It is,
Dear Sister, the one thing we have overlooked
In all our cunningest contrivances.
And I who once contrived so confidently should know that now.
Or do I? Do I yet?

For the old pain comes, the old nerve twitches whenever
Wind shifts, and fitful sits, if only a moment,
In that sweet corner of the heart where once—
No, Sister,
We are betrayed—and always
In the house!

R.P.W.: If you refer to the house Charles Lewis built,
There'll be no more betraying there unless
Spooks betray spooks. And in a spook house, too.
Nothing but rubble, and anyway, to climb
That bluff would daunt the best-conditioned spook.
I climbed it, and I know. It was July.
It's Lucy's monument that gives directions.
They're cut in stone of the obelisk's south face,
And tell you to ascend *the mountain which
Can be seen in the distance one and one
Half miles to northward*, up the Birdville Road.

The owner's name was Boyle, Jack Boyle.
So the mailbox said, outside the whitewashed fence.
The house was white, a tidy bungalow.
The roof was tin, and blazing in the sun,
And zinnias blazed in the one flower bed.
A fat old collie panted in the shade.
I knocked and waited there for Mr. Boyle
To come and tell me I could climb his mountain.
"Sure can," he said, "if you ain't got good sense.
A day like this, and all that brush to fight."

That seemed ungracious, not in country manners,
The only manners left that aren't for show.
But Mr. Boyle was just polite, no more,

And being polite, he hadn't reckoned
To name a man a fool on short acquaintance.
And so he grinned to disinfect the thing,
And said again, more heartily, "Sure can.
But when you git up thar on top
Just one thing, please, just please don't go and bother
My rattlesnakes I'm fattening up for fall."

Oh, he was quaint, was Mr. Boyle,
Or could be made to seem so.
But Boyle's not quaint because he speaks the tongue
His fathers spake, and holds his manners yet.
Or if he's quaint, he's quaint only as a man
Of decent ambitions, country hopes, and did his best,
Mortgage and weather taken to account
And minor irritations flesh is heir to.
Will do his best, no doubt, until he dies,
If he's not dead already, caught the flu, or had
A coronary hit him on the street,
Down in Paducah, where he'd gone to trade.

Alive or dead, Jack Boyle has gone beyond me
And taken with him all the world he made—
Chiaroscuro and brilliance his expert eyeball painted
On all the tolerant emptiness of air.
He's gone and a world's thus dead and gone beyond me,
And part of the world that's dead is I myself,
For I was his creation, too, that fleeting moment
I blocked his doorway and he stared at me,
A fellow of forty, a stranger, and a fool,
Red-headed, freckled, lean, a little stooped,
Who yearned to be understood, to make communication,
To touch the ironic immensity of afternoon with meaning,
While the sun insanely screamed out all it knew,
Its one wild word:
Light, light, light!
And all identity tottered to that remorseless vibration.

Well, after all, I had permission now. So down the road,
In the best shade there was, I parked the car

And left my father drowsing there,
For he was old, already pushing eighty.
No truth on mountains any more for him,
Nor marvel in the bush that burns and yet is not consumed.
Yes, he had climbed his mountain long ago,
And met what face—ah, who can tell?
He will not, who has filled the tract of Time
With rectitude and natural sympathy,
Past hope, ambition, and despair's delectable anodyne.
What face he had met I do not know, but know
That once, in a café in Paris, when an old friend said,
"Tell me about your father," my heart suddenly
Choked on my words, and in that throttlement
Of inwardness and coil, light fell
Like one great ray that gilds the deepest glade,
And thus I saw his life a story told,
Its glory and reproach domesticated.

The failures of our fathers are failures we shall make,
Their triumphs the triumphs we shall never have.
But remembering even their failures, we are compelled to praise,
And for their virtues hate them while we praise,
And praising, wonder, caught in the sudden and corrosive glare
Of speculation like the enemy rocket
Exploding above the torn and terror-bit terrain
Where darkness is the only comfort left—
We wonder, even as we consider their virtue:
What is wisdom and what the dimming of faculty?
What kindliness, and what the guttering of desire?
What philosophic wisdom, and what the fatigue of the relaxed nerve?

But still, despite all naturalistic considerations,
Or in the end because of naturalistic considerations,
We must believe in the notion of virtue. There is no
Inland path around that rock-ragged
And spume-nagged promontory. For past
All appetite and alibi, and past
Your various studies and reasonable ambitions,
Infidelities and chronic self-deception,
And the odor of fresh hay on the night wind

Like the perfume of a woman's parts,
You know that virtue, painful as a syllogism,
Waits, and will wait, as on
The leaf the lethal mantis at his prayer,
And under those great hands, spiked, Gothic, barbed,
Clasped high to arch the summer blue of heaven,
You pass, like ant or aphid in the season's joy, while he,
That green, crank nightmare of the dear green world,
All day, in sun and shade, maintains
His murderous devotion.
For you will come and under the barbed arch meet
The irremediable logic of all the anguish
Your cunning could invent or heart devise.
Or is any answer as complete as that?

Who has seen man in his naked absoluteness?

It was remembering my father that flushed these thoughts.
But now speculation settles like dust
When wind drops, and there is only the great quiet
Of a sunlit space,
For I recall one Sunday afternoon,
How, after the chicken dinner and ice cream,
Amid the comics, and headlines of the world's disaster,
I saw him sit and with grave patience teach
Some small last Latin to a little child,
My brother's child, aged five, and she would say
The crazy words, and laugh, they were so crazy.

There's worse, I guess, than in the end to offer
Your last bright keepsake, some fragment of the vase
That held your hopes, to offer it to a child.
And the child took the crazy toy, and laughed.

I wish you could tell me why I find this scene so sweet.

I left my father in the car to drowse
And went to climb the hill.
Like Boyle had said, I was a fool,
A God-damned fool, and all that brush to fight.

Saw-vine and sassafras, passion-vine, wild rose,
But the roses gone, and bloom of the passion vine,
And blackberry, man-high, dry-snagging for your blood,
And up the bluff, where cedar clambered rock,
The tall, hot gloom of oak and ironwood,
Canted and crazed but tall, and from their boughs
The great grapevine, a century old, hung in its jungle horror,
Swayed in its shagged and visceral delight,
Convolved from bough to bough, halyard, reefline, and forebrace—
The rotten rigging of that foundered hill.

But I went on, and hit the carriage road
Old Lewis' Negroes had chopped from the live rock.
I hoped to God it wasn't in July
Black hands had grabbled and black sweat dropped.
But niggers don't mind heat. At least, not much.
And sure, somebody's got to build the road.
Did I say road? Well, that's an overstatement.
You see the fallen buttressing, that's all,
Poor nigger stonework, generations gone,
And sluicing winter and the oak-root's heave
Have done their duty. So
I damned the saw-briar, slapped the damned sweat-bee.
Went on, and all at once from the last green tangle, burst.

There was the quiet, high glade,
Blue grass set round with beeches, quietest tree.
The air was suddenly sweet, a hint of cool,
I stood in the new silence and heard my heart.
And there it was: the huddled stones of ruin,
Just the foundation and the tumbled chimneys,
To say the human hand, once here, had gone,
And never would come back, though the bright stars
Shall weary not in their appointed watch
And the broad Ohio devotedly seek the sea.
I went up close to view the ruin, and then
It happened. You know,
When you have clambered hard and fought the brush
And breath comes short and both lungs full of cotton,
And shirt is soaked and holds your hide like glue,

23

And heat runs prickling in your blood like ants—
Then if you stop, even in sun-blaze,
It's like malaria shook your bones like dice.

Well, standing there, I'd felt, I guess, the first
Faint tremor of that natural chill, but then,
In some deep aperture among the stones,
I saw the eyes, their glitter in that dark,
And suddenly the head thrust forth, and the fat, black
Body, molten, out-flowed, as though those stones
Bled forth earth's inner darkness to the day—
As though the bung had broke on that intolerable inwardness.
Thus, now divulged, focused, and compacted,
The thing that haunts beneath earth's soldered sill
Flowed forth, and the scaled belly of abomination
Rustled on stone, reared up
In regal indolence and swag.
I saw the soiled white of belly bulge,
And in that muscular distension, the black side scales
Show their faint yellow flange and tracery of white.

It climbed the paralyzed light.

On those heaped stones, taller than I,
Taller than any man,
The swollen head hung
Haloed and high in light; then in that splendid
Nimb the hog-snout parted, and with girlish
Fastidiousness the faint tongue flicked to finick in the sun.

That fastidiousness was, I suppose, the ictus of horror,
And my natural tremor of fatigue
Was converted into the metaphysical chill, and my soul
Sat in my hand and could not move.

But, after all, the manifestation was only natural—
Not Apophis that Egypt feared and the great god
Ra, redemptive, at each dawn slew, but did not slay.
Nor that Nidhogg whose cumbrous coils and cold dung chill
The root of the world's tree, nor even

Eve's interlocutor by Eden's bough.
No, none of these, nor more modestly in Kentucky
The quintessential evil of that ruin,
Nor spirit of the nigger boy named John,
Whose anguish spangled midnight once like stars,
Nor symbol of that black lust all men fear and long for.

No, none of these, no spirit, symbol, god,
Or Freudian principle, but just a snake,
Black Snake, Black Pilot Snake, the Mountain Blacksnake,
Hog-snout or Chicken Snake, but in the books
Elaphe obsoleta obsoleta,
And not to be confused with the Black Racer,
Coluber constrictor—oh, I remember
That much from the old times when, like a boy,
I thought to name the world and hug it tight,
And snake and hawk and fox and ant and day and night
All moved in a stately pavane of great joy
And naked danced before the untouchable Ark of Covenant,
Like Israel's king, and never one fell down.
But when you're not a boy you learn one thing:
You settle for what you get. You find that out.
But if that's all you settle for, you're good as dead.

But to return: old *obsoleta*'s big,
Eight feet—though rarely. But this was big, and he reared
Up high, and scared me, for a fact. Then
The bloat head sagged an inch, the tongue withdrew,
And on the top of that strong stalk the head
Wagged slow, benevolent and sad and sage,
As though it understood our human limitation,
And forgave all, and asked forgiveness, too.

With no haste, it was gone.
This really happened, the big black son-of-a-bitch
Reared from the stones, and scared me, for a fact.
There's no harm in them, though. And they kill rats.

JEFFERSON: Yes, they kill rats. I was a farmer once,
And know. And was a man once too, and know

25

That all earth's monsters are simply innocent,
But one, that master-monster—ah, once
I thought him innocent—

R.P.W.: Innocent?

JEFFERSON: I'm not a fool.
I saw the conduct of life. I saw the things
Men do, broadcloth and buckskin, friend and foe,
And the stench of action is not always sweetened
By the civet of motive, nor motive by good action.
For late at night by the infirm flame I had sat,
While wind walked over Albemarle and sleet
Hissed on the pane, and blood winked
Low in the heart, and I kept my eyes only by
Effort of will on some disastrous page.

R.P.W.: But despite all—

JEFFERSON: Christ's name! I was no fool,
And knew that history drips in the dark.
Listen—there's always a further room,
Where no light is, and the floor would be slick
To your foot. And knew
That if you open the door of the cupboard
There are wood-violet and shanker, *merde* and magnolia, side by side.
And if I thought the housekeeping of Great Nature
Was wasteless and took all to beneficent use,
And decomposition and recomposition are but twin syllables
On the same sweet tongue,
I scarcely held that meditation on the nurture of roses
Is much comfort to a man who has just stepped in dung,
And philosophy has never raised a crop of hair
Where the scalping knife has done its scythe-work.

For I was born in the shadow of the great forest,
And though the slave's black hand bore me, an infant, forth
From that shadow, soft on the silken cushion,
From Shadwell out to Tuckahoe, I always
Carried the shadow of the forest, and therefore thought

That man must redeem Nature, after all,
And if I held man innocent, I yet knew
Not all men innocent,
Ape's tickle and hog's slobber, and the shadow
Of the old trees, for he whom I sent forth
To redeem the wild land to the Western Shore,
My near-son Meriwether, wrote in his papers—

MERIWETHER: Yes, how the savage
Wallowed in the horror of the *hogan*,
And lust is communal ceremony in the murk-filled lodge,
And such the reek of sour bodies and the
Contortion of the bestial face
That nausea was in your gut even as,
For sympathy, your parts twitched.

Yes, laugh at that if you can,
For we are men, and the self
Is what the self is and not
What the self dreams itself to be—and if I once—

JEFFERSON: No, all is not odd, nor all
Even—not if taken in detail. For example,
I had long traveled in fair France, that land
Of sunlight and the sunlit spirit
That once itself shed light on all our faces and whatever
Face, susceptive, lifted to that genial ray,
But there—even there—I saw the abominable relics
Of carved stone heaved up mountain-high by what
Bad energy in what bad time, as though
Chaos had spewed her vomit up in stone, and crazed
Cairns of archetypal confusion, and from every
Porch, pillar, and portal stared
Beaked visage of unwordable evil, and
Fat serpents fanged themselves
To the genitals of women, whose stone eyes bulged out
As to distribute sightlessness on all, and the hacked mouth
Gave no scream you could hear across the long time, and
Vile parodies and mock-shows of the human shape
That might be beasts but yet were men,

Ass-eared, hog-hocked, and buzzard-beaked, and yet
With the human face of slack and idiotic malediction,
Stood about, and
Approved
The sway of the world, and knew, and were, our doom.

I'll tell you a secret—I've met them in the street.
They are a breed
That does not decrease in number or
Significant influence in your own time. Yes, look—
They walk. Shake hands!

MERIWETHER: Yes, yours!

JEFFERSON: Don't sneer. We are each
A child of his own age's womb,
And if then I, bemused by my conception,
Regarded such marvels walking the street as
No more significant than
The depraved ingenuity in stone, merely shade
Of the old lubricity and Gothic night,
Flotsam and frozen foam
Of an ebbed disturbance in Time's tide—
Only the nightmare of a sick child who screamed in the dark,
But no one came—not even the comfort of
Some awkward poor Christ to foot the basilisk
(At Amiens, I think He is). —Ah, once
There was at least the frail
Hope that all monsters of man's begetting may be
Trodden by angels, triumphed on by saints.
But still he screamed.

But then to Nîmes I came, and that Square House—

R.P.W.: I've been to Nîmes—long back, how many years?
There's good wine there, black,
Black as ink—you know, for you once had it there.
Three sous the bottle, you wrote you paid for it.
It costs a lot more now, but worth it still.
I drank the wine, slept in a decent bed,

And the next morning stood in the sun-gilt *place*,
And stared at your "Maison Quarrée."

JEFFERSON: I stood in the *place*. There is no way
For words to put that authoritative reserve and glorious frugality.
I saw the law of Rome and the light
Of just proportion and heart's harmony.
And I said: "Here is a shape that shines, set
On a grundel of Nature's law, a rooftree
So innocent of imprecision
That a man may enter in to find his freedom
Like air breathed, and all his mind
Would glow like a coal under bellows—

R.P.W.: So you find evidence for aspiration
In such a heap of organized rubble
(I call it cold and too obviously mathematical)
Thrown up by a parcel of those square-jawed looters
From the peninsula, stuck in a foreign land?

JEFFERSON: I think I know what the Romans were, know
Better, perhaps, than you, and later, when
A goat let drop his precise pellets, small and black, on imperial mosaic,
And bats clustered, like raisins, in the split vault
Of the *thermae* of some potbellied World Shaker,
Then Rome paid for what Rome was, and—

R.P.W.: Then what of the innocence you find?

JEFFERSON: I referred, my friend, to a time when I once did find it.
And the Square House spoke to my heart of some fair time
Beyond the Roman tax-squeeze, Trimalchio—and then
The Gothic dark. It spoke
Of a time to come
If we might take man's hand, strike shackle, lead him forth
From his own nightmare—then his natural innocence
Would dance like sunlight over the delighted landscape.
Oh, then no saint or angel
To tread down monsters—for man's free foot
Would stamp like vintage in the press,

And laughter, more extravagant than the Burgundian, would racket
Round all the bright pendentives, coigns, and cornices of the sky.

But—

R.P.W.: But?

JEFFERSON: But that
Was *then*, not *now*. Now all
Has been made clear to me, and I know
It is the monsters slain that are innocent—the Hydra,
All hippogrifs and dragons, Grendel and Grendel's dam,
Are innocent. And as for heroes, every one,
The Hercules of hairy thigh, and that David
Who danced his epicene minuet to the tune
Of the sling's twang, and the Cappadocian pig-sticker,
And that square-headed braggart of Hereot, high as the mead-hall,
And Jack of the Beanstalk, too—saints and angels to boot—
But play at sad child's play,
At the old charade where man dreams man can put down
The objectified bad and then feel good.
Ha! the sadistic farce whereby the world is cleansed—
While in the deep
Hovel of the heart the Thing lies
That will never unkennel himself to the contemptible steel.

There was the house, and I will tell you—

II

R.P.W.: Yes, I have read the records, even intended
To make a ballad of them, long ago:

> *The two brothers sat by the sagging fire,*
> *Lilburne and Isham sat by the fire,*
> *For it was lonesome weather.*
> *"Isham," said Lilburne, "shove the jug nigher,*
> *For it is lonesome weather.*
> *It is lonesome weather in Kentucky,*
>
> *For Mammy's dead and the log burns low*
> *And the wind is raw and it's coming snow*
> *And the woods lean close and Virginia's far*
> *And the night is dark and never a star . . ."*

It began about like that, but the form
Was not adequate: the facile imitation
Of folk simplicity would scarcely serve.
First, any pleasure we take in folksiness
Is a pleasure of snobbish superiority or neurotic yearning.
Second, the ballad-like action is not explained,
If explainable at all, by anything in the action.
If at all, it must be by a more complex form, by our
Complicities and our sad virtue, too.

And so to put the story in a ballad
Would be like shoveling a peck of red-hot coals
In a croker sack to tote them down the road
To start the fire in a neighbor's fireplace.
You won't get far with them, even if you run—
No, the form was not adequate to the material.

JEFFERSON: There is no form to hold
Reality and its insufferable intransigence.
I know, for I once thought to contrive
A form to hold the purity of man's hope.

But only dumped hot coals in that croker sack.
The fire burns through, the blood bleeds through, the bowels,
And not of compassion, are pierced, and foulness
Flows forth upon—no, I'll revert to the former metaphor:
If then I had known what I now know,
I had thought it exquisitely better
To seize the hot coals of the human definition
In bare hands, and scream, and run what steps
I could before I fell, and the white
Articulation of hand-bones trellised through
Fire-black flesh.

R.P.W.: It was white bone through black flesh,
Fire-black and nigger-black, that got the brothers
Into their fix. White bone, and a dog that gnawed it.
We do not know what dog—
Some frontier cur slinking the edge of forest,
Or some great brute bred up for bear, or even
One of Lilburne's hounds, perhaps
That beloved Nero from Virginia he named to his father
In his will, the codicil he scribbled the last day
Before he cried aloud and clawed the sod
On his mother's grave.

We have to invent our dog.

We see it liver-spotted, velvet-eared,
With gaze so wise and sad in faithfulness,
Crouched by the trace, on the new grass of spring—
The month is March—and for a background the arabesques
Of leafage dappled with gold, to fret
And freak with joy the dark margin
Of forest. The forest reaches
A thousand miles beyond the frail human project.
But here the trace, and the hound
Crouching with head held high in a hint of heraldic
Nobility, and under the
Forepaws the human bone licked clean, or nearly,
Only some shred of fire-black flesh yet clinging.
        *

What bone? Some bone the passer-by could see
As human, pick up, and take to town.
Tradition says the jawbone of poor John.
Well, put the jawbone of poor John beneath
The forepaws of that hound—

JEFFERSON: The symbolism
Comes most sardonically apt. It was the hound
That Lilburne loved, the only thing alive
He loved, his mother—and my sister—dead.

R.P.W.: Do you really think he loved her? I should say
That his black need requires some other word.

JEFFERSON: Love!
I apologize for introducing that word
In an automatic and old-fashioned way.
No, I'm now ironical at your expense,
Or try to be—which is a way of saying—
Of saying what?

Well, God help me, I'll say it:

I've long since come to the considered conclusion
That love, all kinds, is but a mask
To hide the brute face of fact,
And that fact is the un-uprootable ferocity of self. Even
The face of love beneath your face at the first
Definitive delight—even that—
Is but a mirror
For your own ferocity—a mirror blurred with breath,
And slicked and slimed with love—
And even then, through the interstices and gouts
Of the hypocritical moisture, cold eyes spy out
From the mirror's cold heart, and thus,
Self spies on self
In that unsummerable arctic of the human lot.

R.P.W.: A little back you said you'd used that word *love*
In some impulsive and old-fashioned sense.

Well, I find your present view
Just as old-fashioned as it
Is quaintly nasty.
And begging your pardon, you
Lack a certain pragmatic perspective.

JEFFERSON: What I lack, my friend, is the dream
Of joy I once had, and that,
From the way you talk, I doubt
You ever had.

R.P.W.: All right—for it is scarcely
The most fashionable delusion of my age, and I—
I simply never had it.

JEFFERSON: I did,
And that was joy. Until—

MERIWETHER: Until?

JEFFERSON: Oh, Meriwether—oh, my son—

R.P.W.: You mean until Lilburne—

JEFFERSON: Yes.

MERIWETHER: There had been other and equal fiends, and you,
Not being a child—

JEFFERSON: Not in my blood!
Listen—it is always
The dearest that betrays.

R.P.W.: Oh, yes, the hound!
Symbolically apt, you said.

JEFFERSON: Yes, apt because
We must always be betrayed by the most dear.
Even if the most dear is only a hound.

     *

MERIWETHER (singing):

> *Are these the words I hear him say—*
> *This jolly little miller in his coat of gray?*
> *Oh, rusty-dusty miller,*
> *Dusty was his coat,*
> *Dusty was his color.*
> *Dusty was the kiss I got from the miller!*

JEFFERSON: As I was saying, God help me,
Betrayal may serve justice, for the beloved
Knows well the nature of our love—
Would be avenged for the least love pat and tutelage of fingers,
The imploring pinch in the dark hour, the
Precise concourse of delicate tongue-tips
And the magnanimous act
Of forgiveness—yes, most for that, for that
Is the self's final ferocity
Whetted in sweetness as a blade in oil.

R.P.W.: Lilburne did forgive his wife
In that codicil found
By the body on his mother's grave.
It says: "And to that fair but cruel Letitia,
Whose coldness unto me has brought on all—"

JEFFERSON: Forgave her that he might blame her too!

R.P.W.: Ah, poor Letitia! What a joke of a name
For her to be named Joy.
Even if likely she never knew what the name meant—
The invalid lying upstairs in the dark house, straining
To catch a word of the tangled wrangle below,
Where Isham and Lilburne hunched at the jug,
Summer and winter, and the eavesdropping forest
Leaned in the dark, and no leaf stirred.
Night after night, until—

JEFFERSON: In the December dark—

R.P.W.: The scream—

✻

35

JEFFERSON: It came and filled the room.

LETITIA: And the whole world so dark!
Yet wasn't loud, being
Far off—down in the meat-house, they say—
But I heard it, and then the world
Started screaming too, by itself, like I
Had been waiting for years for it to start, and every
Dead leaf in the woods just screamed like a tongue,
Each little leaf weak, but all together
One big scream filling
My head,
Like one big hollow echo, my poor head big enough
To hold the world, and all the stars,
The stars all screaming.

R.P.W.: And you tried to scream?

LETITIA: But sometimes you can't scream, and a voice
Said *Now!* Like the time had come
You were afraid for, but had to have,
And I knew I had heard that voice in my head before—
The first time ever Lilburne came on me,
And ne'er any man had come before,
But that was terrible, just in its sweetness, but now
This *Now* was terrible just in pure terribleness,
And the next I knew
I was out on the stairs, and was going
To fall. Then, of a sudden,
Was happy, for to fall
Might end whatever there'd been to scream about.

And so I fell.

R.P.W.: But next day got away.
Yes, that's the puzzle, you, an invalid,
Or sort of one. And it's sure Lilburne
Wouldn't let you go and start that talk.

LETITIA: You know how the black folks are, like children.

36

Be nice to them, and they'll be nice to you,
And I was lonesome in that big old house,
And big old bed, so talked to Old Cat
For lonesomeness. She was a good old thing.
And she'd been Lilburne's nigger Mammy, too,
Had nursed him tiddy, and still called him "Chile."
And when my spells came bad, she'd put
Vinegar on my forehead and rub my wrists.
It was Aunt Cat got me away.

Next morning I woke and found myself abed
Where Lil had put me—he'd found me on the stairs—
And Aunt Cat by the bed when first my eyes opened.
So I said: "God, oh, God!" Not loud,
Just to see the room with nothing changed, but different.
Said: "God, I just can't stand it, God."

But didn't know what it was I couldn't stand.

Aunt Cat, she leaned so close I could see
The red lines in her old yellow eyeballs, and yellow
Old broken teeth, and just that second
I didn't know her. And her breath came out, the breath,
It said: "I'll git a hoss."
And I said: "What?"
The yellow eyes came close, and I was scared, but scared
Of what I didn't know, and the breath
Said: "Go!"
I said: "I'm sick." But the breath,
It said: "Hit's the Lawd's last chance. Last night
I heared the Lawd. The yearth shook, I heared him say:
One shall be saved—"

And suddenly, sick at my stomach, it looked
Like I could recollect, and said:
"Last night, did the earth shake—really shake?"
And she: "Chimleys come down, and the water,
Hit sloshed and roared in the river, and the Lawd—"

R.P.W.: This was, of course, December 15, 1811,

37

The night of the great earthquake,
When the Mississippi ran back north three days,
Earth split wide open and moaned like a cow with calf,
And Reelfoot Lake was made, and New Madrid
Fell down, and oak trees snapped like a blacksnake whip.

AUNT CAT: The river, hit slosh and roar, and the Lawd say—

LETITIA: And I marveled slow to recollect.
"Then 'twasn't just my head—the earth,
It shook and threw me down."

And the face was close and awful, and the breath said: "Go!"

And my voice far off, it said: "Yes."

It was Aunt Cat, I knew she loved me, and she said:
"The hoss is saddled, I saddled him, you go!
Afore they knows—and when they knows
Ain't nuthen they can do but beat me—" Then,
Of a sudden: "Lawd, oh, Lawd, jest let 'em
Jest beat me, not nuthen else!"
And I popped up
In that big old bed and saw her face
And I said: "Last night—last night,
Did somebody yell?"

Her eyes, they rolled like nigger eyes will roll.
She looked round quick, said: "Hesh!"
"But somebody yelled!" I said. And she said: "Hesh!
Hit won't be me to tell it, him my Chile."

She helped me get away, she loved me so much.

R.P.W.: She loved you so much, that's one way to put it.
Or hated them, for that's another,
And there's nothing strange
In that, for every act is but a door
Between two rooms, on equal hinges hung
To open either way, on either room,

And every act to become an act must resolve
The essential polarity of possibility,
Yet in the act polarity will lurk,
Like the apple blossom ghostly in the full-grown fruit.
Yet all we yearn for is the dear redemption of
Simplicity.

Can any man wish more than knowledge?
Did that poor fellow Lilburne long for more
When midnight vision burst, and sudden, he saw
The world heave like the forest in a storm,
Heaving
Beneath the blue blaze of the splitting sky,
While darkness danced on tiptoe far above,
And tore
The streaming and apocalyptic horror of its enormous hair?

I refer
Not merely to the earthquake, but also
To that electric moment
When Lilburne knew
At last, at last, the thrilling absoluteness
Of the pure act. Year after year, to have yearned
For the peace of definition. Here it was.

Or near.

So much for Lilburne, but it's now Aunt Cat
We're stuck with—if for love or hate, or both,
She sent Letitia out. She loved her, sure.
But Lilburne, too, she loved.
Oh, yes, she knew Letitia was the one
Sure instrument she had.
So sent her to her brother, sick and gabbling,
Gabbling in terror with no word of fact,
But terror worse than fact, as Aunt Cat knew.
So sent her forth, cocked trap, dug pit,
Fired fox-tail for the Philistine wheat.
She knew the simple classic formula:
Divide the white folks and sit back and wait.

But Aunt Cat still loved Lilburne—yes.
She'd given him suck,
And was his tiddy-Mammy still—

AUNT CAT: I rocked him soft, his stout and bouncen-glad,
And when his belly tight, I pat hit good,
So round and leetle, and I kiss him thar,
Sang, "Lil, my Lilly, Mammy's Baby-Bear."
And he done laugh to git me kiss and sing,
Sing fer the wind to blow and rock him soft,
Sing fer the moon to skeer the Bugaboo,
Sing fer the Cheer-kee never come not nigh
To skeer my punkin Little Baby-Bear,
And no Raw-Head-and-Bloody-Bones to come—
"Raw-Head, Raw-Head, doan come my Honey nigh."
Him sleep by then, and knowed I loved him good,
Fer in Virginny fer, him sleepin sound.

R.P.W.: So now, as I was saying,
And as Cat has documented, it wouldn't be
Her mouth that told the tale.
Just "Hesh" and "Hesh," and who
Could blame Aunt Cat
If Letitia now in her dark, gabbling fear
Could work out her own hate of Lilburne?

LETITIA: Stop!
I love him still.
At least, I guess I do. When I remember
How first I saw him, all the feel comes back
And something in my middle goes all soft
And sort of sick, but a sick all full of sweetness.
Yes, right this minute now when I remember
The first time e'er I saw him.

'Twas Big Court Day,
And folks all came and filled the settlement,
And some the folks that cleared for corn,
And forest folks from where the dark woods are,
All lank and skinny and got deerskin shirts,

And tote their guns and ever walk so sly,
And Indians, too, but not a kind to scare you,
Just poor and dirty and they scratch themselves,
And swamper folks and men from off the river,
With red rags round their necks and whiskers black and wild.
And folks was drinking likker and they sang,
Sang "Barby Allen," sang "Shoot the Buffalo,"
And yelled for fun and made their brags and laughed.
And some were fighting over in the shade.

Who 'twas, I never knew, but came a yell,
It made you shiver, coming so sad and wild.
Then folks, they told
How 'twas a fellow got his eyes gouged out,
The way folks thumb them out when they get fighting.
For mad or fun, it's just the way folks fight.
Who 'twas, they said he bragged and fought for fun.

And I was marveling what a funny yell
And tingly-wild and sweet to make you cry,
And the pretty sunshine he would never see,
For it was spring now, and winter gone and departed.
And I—I felt like crying to see the sun so pretty.

Then I saw Lilburne, not to know his name.
Across the crowd, just sitting his mare.
And sat so easy, too, and limber-like,
Just sitting sideways while he talked,
His left hand on his hip and the right one careless laid
On the mare's curved neck, a-fiddling with her mane.
And when the mare got restless and she danced,
So limber Lilburne's waist just moved with her moving,
And his face was dark and beautiful and still.
And when she danced too much, his hand went strong
Of a sudden on her neck, and—
I felt the hand on my own neck, and I was still.

I just stood weak and shivery in the sun.

But I didn't fall down, I just stood there and loved him,

And didn't know his name, and said right sly
To Sudie Persley standing there beside me—
We girls just stood together like was proper—
So I said: "Sudie, see that funny man,
The man on horseback there so swart and strange?"
I said it that way just to fool her, for I'd
Just die if she knew how I felt.
Oh, she was sly. But she pinched my arm—said: "Silly—
You silly goose, you're flying awful high!
He's Lilburne Lewis lives at Rocky Hill,
Why, he's blood-kin to old Tom Jefferson."

JEFFERSON: Yes, that's the fact that shakes my heart
With the intrinsic shock:
Born of my sister's body, vessel of my blood,
And yet what it is. It was a parcel of flesh
That my sister's body ejected, squeezed out, dropped,
And they cut the cord and trammel
But could not cut the cord that bound her heart
To that unformed flesh. They should have thrown
It out where the hogs come to the holler, out with the swill.

No, I tell you what I should have done
When first I saw it lie on the lace pillow—
You know an infant's face, wizened and seamed
And of no beauty, yet when that parcel of flesh
Is laid on the lace pillow, your heart stirs.
It stirs at a new sense of the human possibility.
Then it seemed to confirm the promise I prayed to live by.

But I tell you, the wizened mark is not the mark
Of new possibility, but is
Prefiguration of the face of vile age,
Where every seam is but the malign
Calligraphy of old indulgences
That glut our time and mark us men.

Yes, truth pocks faces like a foul disease.
Look at my face. Oh, I could tell you
What appetite's crook'd heel here slewed and spurned

And, passing, marked the flesh like mire.
Yes, being old, I am the record of my failure.
But whatever you make of my face, and failure,
I reject, repudiate,
And squeeze from my blood the blood of Lilburne and—

LUCY: Brother, I beg you,
For the sake of your own soul and salvation—

JEFFERSON: But I'd have at least a soul
If not salvation.

LUCY: Oh, Brother, how sweet he lay to my arms!

JEFFERSON: Listen, when some poor frontier mother, captive, lags
By the trail to feed her brat, the Indian,
He'll snatch its heels and snap
The head on a tree trunk, like a whip,
And the head pops like an egg. Well,
There wasn't any tree, it being indoors, but the brickwork
Of the chimney would have been perfectly adequate.

Now truly, dear Sister, don't you wish I had done it?

LUCY: In God's name—

JEFFERSON: Well, I scarcely imagine
That John, the black boy, would share your views.
Or for that matter, Letitia,
Sick and shivering on the horse to flee.

LETITIA: I just hung on, hung on the best I could.
To the settlement, and my brother came,
And again the world shook, and folks named the End of Time.
They prayed. But I just prayed for the End.

R.P.W.: It takes something more to bring the End of Time
Than that Roman circus in your meat-house.
That was just an episode in the long drift of human
Experience, and impressive chiefly for

Its senselessness. And there's always
Enough coiling miasma
From the fat sump of common consciousness
To make any hour perfectly appropriate
For Gabriel's tootle.
The folks, for instance, who fell down
Right in the road and prayed couldn't have any idea
Of the meat-house. For each man has
A different set of well-fondled reasons
To make any hour seem perfectly made to order
For God's wrath.
As this present hour would seem
To any of us right now if earth shook and sky darkened—
That is, if we weren't so advanced
Beyond the fear of God's wrath.

LETITIA: I wasn't afraid of what the Lord might do.
I was afraid of what he might not do.
I rolled my head on the pillow there and prayed
For the End of Time—after all that had happened to me.

R.P.W.: Now what I can't understand
Is how something didn't happen quick to Lilburne.
Your brother must have guessed something,
And even if the Lewises were great—

BROTHER: Look here, there won't be that kind of talk.
No man e'er said I was afraid, Lewis or not.
Just let a man
Do something to my sister he hadn't ought to,
And I'd know why, and they don't come too big.
You give me a reason—
And I'd step right up and pull Jesus Christ off the cross
And make Him talk turkey even if folks do say
His Pappy is a big man in the home section.
Lewises, hell. A Lewis ain't got but two balls
And hung in the same place like anybody else.

Oh, he was polite and never uppity.
Just once a man gets uppity with me.

He'd name me "Brother," sweet as pie,
But there was something 'bout him, hard to say.
The way his face was—

LETITIA: Oh, it was still but it was beautiful!

BROTHER: Well, that's sort of laying it on.
Sometimes his eyes
Just stared at you so bright with a kind of shine,
Like he was looking through you—

LETITIA: Oh, yes—his eyes. I felt I'd just fall down.
At least it was that way the first I knew him.
It was the Persley house where we first talked,
Before the big in-fare when Sudie wed.
And when the fiddles took up high and clear
To give the reel and make the folks all happy,
The music was all sparkly-bright like fire,
And burning in me spangly in the dark,
And Lilburne took my hand and my breath was short.

BROTHER: He had a way to look at a man sort of
Like you weren't there,
And ain't no man gonna—

LETITIA: Oh, I was nothing—
Just nothing when he looked, and I wanted to be
Just nothing and him everything, but me
A nothing that somehow was part of every
Sweet part of him,
Like air he breathed and didn't know or heed,
Or maybe water he was swimming in,
But I'd just hold him up, and be round him everywhere.

R.P.W.: But then—

LETITIA: Just how it started I don't know. It wasn't
A thing to lay a name to, and I reckon
There's just no name to lay to the worst thing.
                *

But it's awful not to know what the worst is,
For if you don't know that, I reckon
You don't know anything.
Then, God,
My living was just plain nothing, God.
Oh, even if You're God and take a mind
With one big huff-and-puff
To blow the moon and stars across the sky,
Like a boy just blowing dandelion fuzz,
Or grab the sun and squeeze it in your hand
And the sky all dark, forever—

Oh, God, even if You're God, you haven't got
The right to make me not know anything,
And what it means, and why,
And not be nothing, God.
I don't ask much, just to know what it all came to, God.

R.P.W.: You don't ask much. Just everything,
Or maybe the one thing God can't give.
Or anybody.
All you demand is definition, too,
Just like poor Lilburne. Do you hate him less
To think that he, like you—

LETITIA: Oh, I don't hate him!

R.P.W.: As I was saying, do you hate him less
To think that he, like you, might have been only trying
To know what the good thing was, and when
He couldn't know that, then did the worst,
Whatever the worst thing was, he did to you?

LETITIA: Oh, I don't know what the worst thing was,
Or whether it just sort of happened to him, too.

He could be so sweet—oh, yes! That is, sometimes.
Like once we rode in the woods and it was fall,
And sunshine bright and trees bright-colored,
And one big sweet-gum golder than the sun,

And he rode up and stood high in his stirrups
To pull a piece and cut it with his knife,
And held it in his hand, and looked at me.
You know how sweet-gum is, the leaves like stars?
Like stars all gold, and he held them in his hand.

Then, "Stop!" he said, and pushed my cape-hood back,
Then slow and careful, leaf by leaf, he put
Stars all around, stuck in my hair.
Then leaning back to look, he said:
"Your hair's all gold, Letitia, gold, and now
The stars are in it, gold. I put them there."

My hair's not gold, just sort of washy-brown,
But it felt sweet to hear him name it gold,
And say: "Oh, you're an angel from the sky!"

And he was smiling like I never saw.

But *puff*! and the candle out,
His face was dark, he grabbed my wrists, and leaning
Close to my face, said: "If you're an angel,
Then I simply give you one piece of advice:
Go!"

And watched my face, and laughed right short,
And said: "Go back to Heaven if you can,
And if you can't, then try the Other Place,
For"—and flung my wrists down hard—
"I tell you, even Hell would be better than this sty."

And rode on then and never said a word.

And night came on, and I lay in the dark alone,
With Lilburne gone, nor tarry for supper even.
But midnight, I heard him come
From down at the settlement, at the tavern there.

R.P.W.: So that's the worst, you say?
    *

47

LETITIA: Oh, no! And different, too. And worse.
I reckon I just started telling this
So as not to think about the other, just
To forget I've got to tell it too.
The words, they grow in me, they hurt to come.
But you can't forget, not anything that happens,
For forgetting is just another kind of remembering.
No, that sounds silly. But it's crazy-true.
The way when the bad thing comes, and you cry out:
"Oh, no—this can't be me! For I'm Letitia.
I'm Little Tishie—" and I played beside the river
And sang a song to make the river run,
And I minded Momma, and when the sun got low,
She called, and I took my doll and went.

They named me Tishie. I was little then.

How can you believe it's you things happen to?
But I heard Lilburne
Out there on the stair, and I knew
Why he'd come back from down in the tavern there.
For when Mother Lewis was alive
Lilburne just drank in the tavern if his blues came on.
But then came back.
He was good to her, always.

LUCY: Yes, always to me—
And if there is love at all, oh, Letitia,
If only a grain, no matter
The kind or shape, it is precious.

But I made the repudiation. I died.

LETITIA: But that was another night—and now
I heard Lil on the stair, in the dark,
And didn't know what would happen, but something.
Like at night, in the woods, lost,
You wait to hear it breathe,
Or paw move.
               *

48

Then heard him breathe. And say:
"Do you love me, Letitia?"
And I whispered, "Yes"—
Yet my voice was thin, like somebody far.
His voice said "Ah!" in the dark.

Then he did it.

And it was an awful thing
I didn't even know the name of, or heard tell—
I'd plain forgot—
It was so awful that folks could do so awful.
But when he did it, even if I'd never heard,
It came just like an awful remembering,
Like it had happened long back, not now, not now,
And I wanted to yell "Stop!" But couldn't,
For if a thing is like an awful remembering
That comes from you deep inside, then you can't say "Stop,"
For it's already happened, it's you.

And Lilburne—you know I loved him,
No matter how awful that folks could do so awful.
And I—why, I—

BROTHER: Look here, if you just told me,
I'd stopped his clock, for ain't no man, nobody,
Going to do dirty to my sister, no matter
What kind of dirty and—

R.P.W.: So that was the worst, Letitia?

LETITIA: Why, no. There was next day to come.
Next day, sunset and we sat by the fire,
The night coming on, and the gray light filling the land,
For today it was clouds, not like
When sunshine made sweet-gums all gold,
And what happened had happened.

Not a word now to say, and I saw out the window,
Down the bluff and over the flat land, far off

Where the river gave off a cold light,
Like a knife in shadow and the blade
Gives off a light with a gleam-like, so still and cold.
And I tried not to think but be still,
Like the land and the gray light.

But Lilburne said: "Don't you love me, Letitia?"
Oh, what could I say! For I loved him, I loved him, no matter.
So I said yes. And he pulled his chair close,
Took my hand to kiss it, and kissed it. And said:
"My poor Letitia, I love you." And what could I say?
For all things that ever had happened were only a dream now,
And this was the real—the realness his mouth on my hand
And the firelight dancing so pretty in the dark room.

But my lips wouldn't move.

And he rose up, rose high, and looked down.
Steady, till I was nothing:
Nothing but sweetness—for his face, it was smiling,
And smiling the smile that always brought sweetness,
And whispering low, said:
"Last night—remember?"

And my heart, it stopped.
Like when you step in the dark and nothing is there,
For it happened again in my head, and might happen forever.

But I said: "Yes."

And he: "Ah." Said "Ah."
Said: "Letitia—now tell me exactly what happened."
And crouched at my side.

But my words wouldn't come and my poor chest was a bigness
That hurt like something swelled there, and I cried:
"I can't, I just can't!"
He jerked away, said:
"Oh, you never loved me, not ever!"
And rose up, his arms flung wide

Like he wiped the world away.

So I cried out: "Oh, Lilburne—I love you!"

He stared down at me, said just one word. Said: "Love."

And the word like he spat it out from his mouth,
Like spit hawked up and cold on your tongue and you spit it,
And I saw the word on the floor,
On the board like a glob to quiver and glimmer a gleam-like,

And the word—it was *love*.

I saw the word there, so slimy and cold.
Cried out, before my heart would break:
"Oh, Lil—I'll say it!"

And he said: "Ah."

And took my wrist to hurt, he was so strong,
And squatted there, and the fire fell low.
Said "Ah," and leaned, and the last fire lit his face.
And the bigness that in my chest had hurt me so
And was not words, was words now, and they came,
And some were words I never named before,
They were so awful, nor heard tell—

Then words were over and done,
Like rain or wind had stopped, and now I'd sleep,
For all that had happened that night before, or ever,
It seemed so far, and little-like, and sad,
And I could sleep forever on Lilburne's shoulder,
Forever dark and quiet and day not come.

But close he leaned, his eyes were shining
Their deepest shine, and he said: "Angel."
Said: "Angel, you've told me all.
But one thing more:
Now didn't you like it then?
And even now to tell me?"
                *

My cheeks got hot, my breath
Was gone like I was dead, but, far away,
A voice was saying "Yes"—so weak and strange.

And oh, I wanted to sleep.

"But, Angel," said Lilburne, "just yesterday,
You were an angel and your hair was gold,
And golden stars in it, I put them there.
But now—"

And sudden rose up from my side,
And stood up tall like he would fill the room,
And fill the house maybe, and split the walls,
And nighttime would come pouring in like flood—
Oh, he was big, and way up there
Like 'twas the darkness of an awful sky,
His eyes were shining, but they shone so dark.

Listen—you know how when the locust goes
And his skin is left, a little shell of him,
So thin and dry and like a little ghost,
And light moves through it and the hollowness
So hollow it is nothing. That was me.

And way above, Lil's face, it swung,
And his voice said: "—but now I see when angels
Come down to earth, they step in dung, like us.
And like it."

And laughed out loud and long.
Then gone. And me alone,
While the fire died down, and me
All thin and dry, and through my hollowness
The dark and air might move and nothing be
But me—me nothing in my hollowness.

BROTHER: God-a-Mighty, and you just never told me nothing.
He 'bused you and you laid up nigh a durn year
Before you broke and left. And then, God-durn,

You moaned and jabbered, and talked no sense,
Nor told me how he 'bused you in the bed.
If you told me, I'd stopped his clock.
Lewises, hell! Ain't nothing to a Lewis
Airy man ain't got, and him a man, and me—
And me, by God, I'm much a man
As airy Lewis ever skinned a pecker,
Me—Billy Rutter—and by God, no man
Will do my sister dirty—

LETITIA: Oh, your sister!
It's not your sister—me—you care about!
Oh, sure, you'd kill my Lilburne if you knew,
Brag in the tavern how you killed a Lewis,
And how no man could do your sister dirty.
Your sister!—Oh, not for love of me
You'd hurt my darling Lil—

But Lil, oh, God!
He put the stars in my hair and called me angel
And said he loved me,
But love is the way lips move and a terrible sound.
And folks do what they do, and call it love.

He rose up high, his face hung there.
I thought the house would split and night flood in.
Said what he said, how angels step in dung.
And three days drunk in the settlement,
And beat the boy that Mother Lewis sent
To fetch him home—the nigger boy named John.

Poor John got back, he hung to the doorjamb there,
Blood on his face, and nigger blood
It's brighter than white folks' blood.
And Mother Lewis, she called out "God!"
But not a word from John, him too far gone.
And she, she stared. Then reached one finger, slow,
To touch the blood.

LUCY: To touch it, and the terribleness

Of knowledge. My mind
Was saying the pure and simple thing,
The sort of thing to live by and make the day good,
Saying: *This boy is hurt,*
Get water, bathe his blood, bind up the wound.
But I could not move to execute the good thing.
And that is strange—when faculty is frozen.
Ah, had I got the water, bathed the wound,
Then everything—oh, that small obligation
Fulfilled might have swayed the weight of the world.

I stood and saw the black face blown with pain.
I saw the irrevocableness of the gaze fixed on me.
I saw my hand move out, weightless and witless and slow,
To glimmer white through the dark and thickening air.
And there was nothing else in my mind left,
Like a wet sponge passed over a child's slate.

JEFFERSON: Yes, dear Sister, your hand reached out to touch
The brightness of violent blood, and in that moment
All values are abrogated in blankness, like
A child's slate swabbed.

LUCY: That blood—why, I knew it was only a dream!

MERIWETHER: Just your evilest dream.

LETITIA: That finger—it moved so slow
I thought that it would never—

LUCY: I knew if I touched
And found it nothing but air—

R.P.W.: But it wasn't.

JEFFERSON: Why didn't you strike? Yes, strike that face
Whose pain was reproach and insult?
For if your fist, dear Sister, finds flesh
You will know a rush of wild joy.
What's a fist for? And you—

54

You are only human.
You're Lilburne's mother, aren't you?

LUCY: Hush, Brother, hush, it was simply
I prayed it was only a dream—

JEFFERSON: But touched—

LUCY: And cried out: "God!" And suddenly,
Time flowed back.
Flowed back and over. It whirled me like a flood.

LETITIA: So she just fell down flat there on the floor.
We put her in the bed, and now sent Isham
Down to the settlement to fetch Lil home.
He came and stood at the bed-foot, quiet,
Not drunk now, weak and pale, and her eyes came open,
But not a word—

LUCY: I saw his face,
But a wide world between, like a valley,
And his face gone small in distance,
And the rain fell steady between,
The distance but to the bed-foot but great as forever,
And the face yearned toward me across the valley,
And my heart made a cry: "Oh, God!
I will go back and endeavor anew
The blessedness of the human obligation."

But the rain fell steady. Then when
It no longer contrived its consistent whisper,
I knew
I was dead.

LETITIA: Yes, she was dead, but we—
We didn't know. Just Lilburne knew. His breath
Came like a gasp, like what last breath
She had breathed out, he'd just sucked in.

I saw him—something on his face

Was growing like darkness when the moon sinks down.
I knew, like ice: *He knows she's dead.*
But we don't know—he knows because her dying
Is his own dying, too. And look! he's dead.

And wanted to yell out: *Oh, please, oh, Lil, don't die!*

Then Father Charles, he leaned across the bed
And with his thumb and finger, sly and sleight,
Like you'd pick up a pin, he picked up slow
Her eyelid edge, and leaned the candle nigh.

And the eyeball showed its white in the candle flame.

He dropped the eyelid, and that little motion
Seemed awful to me—awful, like
With that one little motion of his finger
He'd let her fall, and she would fall forever
Where stars don't come, and even God's afraid.

He dropped the eyelid like you close a book,
All reading done, and set the candle by.
I saw his mouth was quivering
Set in that face as still as sunken stone.
But it made a sound. The sound, it was: "She's dead!"

"You're right," said Lilburne, "and it was you—"
He stopped and stared his pappy in the face.

You've heard the stillness when the wind stops sudden.
You've heard the gunshot, then how still
With a little wist of smoke hung at the muzzle
And no wind stirs it, it frazzle-blue and pretty.
The room was still. I saw his pappy's face, and thought:
We're all dead here, and ain't no use to live.

The old man, he lifted up his hand. It shook.
He held it out like he would beg. He said:
"My boy, my boy." And that was all he said.
            *

But Lilburne: "Yes, you killed her, you did that.
Oh, she loved Albemarle. You brought her here,
And woods are dark and the river stinks all summer,
And the world's a sty, and the world all stinks and stews,
Oh, she loved Albemarle—she was my mother—"

And Lil was crying then. The tears ran down.

I saw him cry, but couldn't stir nor budge.
He looked so little, who had been so big.
He looked so weak, and him so strong and stout.
I saw the tears.
But I couldn't budge.

If just I touched him, just a finger-weight.
Or named his name, named "Lil," so sweet and low.
Then all might different be, and all
Night long he'd lie and sleep inside my arm,
Him breathing sweet beside, and ne'er
A rooster crow for meanness nor for spite,
To end the dark where I would smell his hair.
But I couldn't budge.

R.P.W.: In other words, you couldn't,
To put the matter succinctly, forgive Lilburne.

LETITIA: Forgive? Forgive? It wasn't not forgiving.
It was just I couldn't budge, and the world was ice.
It was Aunt Cat who—

R.P.W.: It was Aunt Cat who what?

LETITIA: She saw Lil's tears run down.
And took his hand, and said: "Oh, Lil, my Honey—"
Like he was little, like the times gone by
When he was little and she nursed her Chile.

AUNT CAT: I nursed him good, and him my Chile and Honey.
Tiddy I give him, tiddy, and loved him good.

LETITIA: The tears ran down, then Cat, she took his hand.
Said: "Lil, my Honey, come on, git to bed."
Said: "Chile." Said: "Chile." And him so drooped and slow.
Till nigh the door. Said: "Chile, yore Mammy's dead.
But I'm yore Mammy, too. I give you tiddy."

Lil stopped, then swung round wild,
And stood. Then leaned right in Cat's face:
"All right, I sucked your milk, but now—"

And stopped.

And Cat said: "Chile."

"But now," he said, "I'd puke the last black drop,
I'd puke it out— Oh, God, my mother's dead!"

He spat there on the floor.
And the room was still, and the dead one on the bed.
And Cat, she cried. Her tears, they came.

R.P.W.: Yes, it was monstrous, what he did, all right.
But in a strange way somewhat justified.
Oh, no—nothing can justify the essential cruelty of—

LETITIA: She loved him, that was all.

R.P.W.: She loved him, sure,
But that's not all, for even love's a weapon.
Let's take the situation.
Now, anybody raised down home—down South—
Will know in his bones what the situation was.
Yes, she would struggle
For Lilburne's love, for possession of her Chile.
But the enemy, the rival, Lucy Lewis.
The rival had the armament and power:
The natural mother, warm and kind—and white.
The rival whose most effective armament
Is the bland assumption that there is no struggle—
Nor can be—between the white love and the black.

58

A struggle, dark, ferocious, in the dark
For power—for power empty and abstract,
But still, in the last analysis, the only
Thing worth the struggle.

This much Cat knows,

And knows she has one weapon, only one.
It's love. So when the mother's dead,
Cat's love is proclamation and triumph
Over the fallen adversary. No wonder
That Lilburne strikes in rage, and outrage, back.

But still, Cat loved him, and that love is valid,
As even Lucy would admit—and to be prized.
This isn't a cynical joke, oh, no.

And Lilburne—

LETITIA: He walked the woods, and it was dark.
We called, we called, but his dog barked far away.
So late, so late, I lay in my bed and waited,
And felt in the dark how Time moves by,
Nor never knows your name, or looks to notice you.

Then out of the woods and darkness, there was Lil,
And laid his head dark down.
"And, oh," he said, "my mother's gone!"
And tears came out and wet me through my gown.
I wanted to feel something, but just couldn't.
Or felt too many things, all different,
But my hand, like by itself, would pat his head in the dark.

Can you tell me why I never felt a thing?

R.P.W.: What could it have changed, a gush of feeling?
Both you and Lucy choose to torture that question,
To assume that some difference in tone or gesture
Would have changed—
        *

LUCY: Oh, no,
The heart, a difference in the heart.

JEFFERSON: Nothing would change nothing!
For Lilburne would ingurgitate
All you'd give, all hope, all heart, all—
Disbursed down that rat hole.

Nothing would change.

III

R.P.W.: Lilburne was Lilburne, and the year drove on.
They buried Lucy Lewis in the yard.
Winter: and from the Dakotas
Wind veers, gathers itself in ice-glitter
And star-gleam of dark, and finds
The long sweep of the valley.
A thousand miles and
The fabulous river is ice in the starlight.
The ice is a foot thick, and beneath,
In the interior of that unpulsing blackness
And thrilled zero, the big channel-cat, eye lidless, hangs
With white belly brushing
The delicious and icy blackness of mud.

But there is no sensation. How can there be
Sensation when there is perfect adjustment? The blood
Of the creature is the temperature of the sustaining flow:
The catfish is in the Mississippi and
The Mississippi is in the catfish and
Under the ice both are at one
With God.

Would that we were!

Wind rises. Even the deep
Intimacy of the thicket shudders. The last burr that clung
On the chestnut bough surrenders, the last haw-fruit,
And what crimson berry of dogwood the possum has spared
Falls now, in the hour past pain, of the relaxed tendon.

Far north the great conifers darkly bend and unburden
Their dignity of snow, and the stridor
Rises to anguish. The oak
Stands on a headland above an enormous curve of the river.
It has stood there two hundred years. The trunk is iron.
The oak's comment is anguish, but

All night, like Jacob, it wrestles the
Pitiless angel of air. The stars are arctic, and
Their gleam comes earthward down
Uncounted light-years of disdain,
And the continent
Glitters whitely in starlight like a great dead eye of ice.
The wind is unceasing, and the stars likewise.

Why do we feel the necessity to linger on this scene?
The answer, I hazard, is paradoxical.
We feel that the force now driving Lilburne on
Is but part of the unhoused force of Nature,
Mindless, irreconcilable, absolute:
But we also feel a need to leave that house
On the headland, and lift our eyes up
To whatever liberating perspective,
Icy and pure, the wild heart may horizonward command,
And so the glimmering night scene under
The incalculable starlight serves
As an image of lethal purity—
Infatuate glitter of a land of Platonic ice.

It is an image to free us from the human trauma.

The walls of the house are deep-notched, but
The candle flame shudders on the wick. The wind
Has found the chimney, sparks
Eddy the hearth. "Isham,"
Says Lilburne, "shove me the God-damned jug."

For, long since, jug has replaced decanter and Madeira.

Letitia lies upstairs. The slaves
Are in their quarters, snug as varmints,
Save John, who drowses by the kitchen fire,
Waiting to help his master up to bed.
And, as for Father Lewis, he is gone.
Back to Virginia, back where—

CHARLES: Can it matter

62

Where wanders the emptiness of air?
Even in that time when still I paid my taxes,
Transacted business, gorged and voided bowels,
And was an identity defined in the temporal eye—
Even then, as I recollect, I was sometimes surprised
To see that my boot left print in dust or damp earth.
To Kentucky I had come to seek my reality.
But in Kentucky I had lost the one person
To whom I was real. But the loss, I must confess,
Was ambiguous. There was, of course, my sorrow.
Relief, also. Relief that I was no longer
In need to strive to be worthy of her love:

Ah, the terrible burden of love!

We buried her
Alone in the wild earth, and my heart said: *Oh, Lucy,*
My Lucy, rot to nothingness, enter
The depth of nothingness, rot
Into the postulated oblivion,
That in nothing we may at long last love
In appropriate mutuality, nothing
To nothing.

And turned away and took the long road home,
Over the mountains, far away,
And in that action equivalently said:
May my seed rot and the fruit of your womb.
I leave them unto darkness and the dark land.
I have looked in the eyes of my son and seen
The landscape of shadow and the shore of night.
Let him fulfill my destiny. Farewell.

And took my leave, and waited for the end.

R.P.W.: So Lilburne's now alone. They have left him now,
Mother and father, wife, and old Aunt Cat.
For if wife and Cat are in the house,
Their faces turn, they drift like shadow past,
And Lilburne knows that he's repudiated.

There's Isham—he is there, I'd nigh forgot—
But only a mirror for Lil's loneliness.
There's some excuse, therefore, for Lilburne's wild wail
Of loneliness, when he first appeared to us,
And his complaint of desertion in the dark.
But we may say, with logic, it was he
Who did the repudiating, who cast forth
Them all. That's true. But even so,
We must remember that always the destroyer
It is who has most need of love: therefore destroys.
And in the unity of life remember
That destruction's but creation gone astray,
That life and death both enter by a wound,
And in the eternal paradox of powers
The oldest ritual instructs us how
The sad God rises
In season past the pathos.
And I once read in Bernard of Clairvaux
How the wicked man, even in wickedness,
But seeks God, after all.

JEFFERSON: But the fact is always the fact—

R.P.W.: And the year drives on.
Now is the hour of iron: accept the obligation,
And the sap of compassion withdraws uttermost inward
To sleep in the secret chamber of Being.
Where is that chamber? And the year drives on.

And now is a new year: 1811.
This is the *annus mirabilis*. Signs will be seen.
The gates of the earth shall shake, the locked gate
Of the heart be struck in might by the spear-butt.
Men shall speak in sleep, and the darkling utterance
Shall wither the bride's love, and her passion become
But itch like a disease: scab of desire.
Hoarfrost lies thick in bright sun, past season,
And twitches like wolf fur.

The call of the owl discovers a new register.

64

When ice breaks, the rivers flood effortlessly,
And the dog-fox, stranded on the lost hillock,
Barks in hysteria among the hazel stems.
Then the bark assumes a metronomic precision.
The first water coldly fingers
The beast's belly. Then silence. He shudders, lets
The hind quarters droop beneath the icy encroachment.
But the head holds high. The rigid
Muzzle triangulates the imperial moon.
Until the spasm, the creature stares at the moon
With the aggrieved perplexity of a philosopher.

Sullen, the waters withdraw. Mud crusts the high
White boughs of the sycamore. Slime
Crusts the creek-flats.
It is green like velvet. Sickness begins in June.
Strong men die willingly.
Breath shakes the pole-shanty.
Dog-days, and stars fall, and prayers have ceased.
Men had come West in hope. This is the West.

Therefore, what more is there to hope for?

The arrogant comet shoulders the old constellations.
It comes too late, men now past fear or wonder:
From clearing or keelboat only a dull eye observes.
Night after night and it sheds a twilight of shuddering green
Over the immensity of forest. The beasts
Of the forest participate in the peculiar dislocation.
Habit and courage of kind change, and lust
Out of season, and lust for strange foods, as when
Rome shook with civil discord, and therefore beasts,
Augustine says, kept not their order, for the wild
Clang of that untunement echoed in all things.
Squirrels flee South, but cannot cross the Ohio.
They drown there, by thousands. Their bodies bloat on the sand bars.
The wild pigeon migrates early this year.
Their droppings have a strange odor, and men
With nausea reject this once-esteemed fowl,
The worst is to come yet, when the earth shall shake.

IV

R.P.W.: But not yet, and life proceeds at Rocky Hill.
All spring you can look from the bluff-head, and see
Waters subside too late for corn. But grass,
Sparse and tentative, sprigs the raw earth
Of Lucy's grave, and Lilburne comes from the house.
He comes, in broad daylight, softly,
Like lecher or thief, foot on unsounding earth.
Why should there be a nagging pain at the left groin?
He must have strained himself with a slut at the settlement.
He was drunk, and cannot
Recall clearly.
Letitia had refused him. Well, that's that.

Now he stares at the new grave, raw, and the pain nags.
April: the grave here six months now, and the grass
Now makes the first green gesture of reclamation.
On the mound, slightly eroded by winter,
Each blade of grass is isolated, and pale
With April's pale perfection,
Protruding, lost, from that earth's intolerable rawness.

Nor can he bear
The sight of the grass. He knows that when that vernal
Mitigation comes back, he
Will be deprived of something,
Of some essential reality. The sight
Of the wounded earth—he craves it, craves
Pain, sorrow, the oppression of breath.
Ah, that's reality!

If the grass comes back, then what, what will be left?
His heart
Floods dear with desolation.
Why does he suffer, and understand nothing?
            *

66

At this moment, now, the favorite hound approaches.
Tail down, or wagging slightly, the pace slow.
Nero stands by the master, and the mournful
Head lifts to gaze with uncritical sympathy.
The hound licks the down-hung hand of the master.
But the tongue's sweetness on flesh
And the gaze of brute affection touch some trigger
Deep in the master's being, some reflex of desperation.
Lilburne kicks the hound savagely in the side.

The act surprises him, himself. The hound
Has been bowled over. It does not flee. It crawls
Drag-belly on the grass, to Lilburne.
It knows there has been some terrible mistake.
There had been no mistake.
This time, with great deliberation, Lilburne kicks.
The hound shuts eyes and shivers, takes the blow.
Then flees, and Lilburne stands there
Dazed, in the April sunlight of
The Year of Wonders.

Later, in shame, he seeks the hound. The hound
Forgives him, licks his hand, but Lilburne
Feels no joy. He would like to feel
The ineffable joy of the soul's restoration.

That night he strikes a slave. The transgression
Had not been great. A cup broken
That Lucy Lewis habitually had used
For morning tea. The thing spoke no great value,
And the breaking, too, was accidental.
The slave protests, for in the Lewis house
All discipline has been in
Each day's easy justice. *Protests*: that's his mistake.
Next morning whipped, and that with Lilburne by
To count the strokes, assess the proper force.
It's John again, a boy just turned sixteen.
Then Lilburne rides down to the settlement
To take his joram; and scarcely round the bend
When John lights out. His world's all upside down.

Can't stand it. Cuts for the woods. The second mistake:
For where, in those days, could a nigger run?
Starvation or the scalping knife, that's all.
So belly-growl or reflection on the transience
Of the human topknot might send the fellow home.
That is, if still he had topknot to noggin.
So home to take his stripes.

Violence breeds cunning, and cunning
Violence, and the first cup in innocence broken
Is succeeded by a dozen broken by design.
But who has broken them? Nobody knows.
They just aren't there any more, on hook or shelf.
Spoons disappear. Where do they go?
It doesn't matter to the people now
It's Ole Miss's cup—Miss Lucy's cup or spoon.
They'd loved Miss Lucy—or if the word *love*
Sounds too much like old Thomas Nelson Page
To sit easy on our stomachs salivated with modernity,
Then we can say that in the scale of subordination,
The blacks, those victims of an obsolescent
Labor system (we can't, you see, just say
"Immoral labor system," for that
Wouldn't be modern, except for people
Who want things both ways)—well, the blacks
Had been conditioned, by appeals to the ego,
To identify themselves with the representative
Of the superordinate group, i.e., the mistress—
In other words, they liked her "tol-bul well."
Might say: "Ole Miss, she know a nigger feel."
And if that is not love, then it's something that will do.

Yes, they would have defended all her spoons against
The Powers of Darkness and Old Scratch Himself
With reasonable loyalty, if it came to a tight,
But now she is dead.
And so they come to hate her, too, that instant
The cup splits on the stone, or the spoon whitely
Glimmers to die in the dark deep of water?
They'd have to hate her, too, to justify.
                    *

Spoons, cups—a man just can't keep track.
A woman might. Letitia, if she weren't sick.
Yes, any woman might. She might surprise
Dish-washing or table-setting, and make her audits,
And still not be regarded as a monster in the kitchen.
They'd say: "Ole Miss—you know, she jes lak dat."

But in a man
It's monstrous, out of nature, for a man
Just doesn't know the rules of such a game.
If in the middle of the afternoon,
Lilburne, just day-drunk and not night-drunk yet
(Day-drunk—a stage known only by a slight
Up-twitching of the left corner of the mouth),
Comes to stand in the middle of that dark
Cave of the kitchen, where eye-whites roll and gleam,
And says: "I want to see my mother's spoons!"—
Always one gone.

Always somebody gets hurt.

But Lilburne most. He feels that something
Terrible is happening to his mother.
They are making the grass come back
On that raw earth of her grave, the flesh
Fall off her bones, changing
The expression of her face. By God, he'll stop it!
But nothing can impede the secret hand,
Black thumb on white china, on silver, a single
Black finger fastidiously plucking flesh from face-bone.
He does not see these images, he only feels them.

And feels the eyes that spy—

JEFFERSON: Spy!—they spy from the shadow.
They serve you the dish and stand with face blandly
Averted, but sidewise that black picklock gaze
Triggers the tender mechanism
Of your secret being.
Oh, they've surprised you

At meat, at stool, at concupiscence,
And when you turn inward,
At the heart's darkest angle you meet
The sly accusation and the shuttered gleam—
Sidewise, of course.

R.P.W.: I begin to think
You're finding some sort of justification for Lilburne.

JEFFERSON: Listen, you can hear nothing, for
Their feet come soft,
Come softlier than silence,
And innocence will avail nothing—I tried
To be innocent, but the eyes—

R.P.W.: Were there. And don't forget you lived
In the lean, late years by the skill of some colored mechanics,
Nailmakers, I think, that luckily you'd trained up.
Well, this is impertinent, but to build Monticello,
That domed dream of our liberties floating
High on its mountain, like a cloud, demanded
A certain amount of black sweat.

MERIWETHER: Look! There it floats!
Against the heavens' blue—that cloud of your dream!

JEFFERSON: I lived in the world.
Say that. But say, too, that I tried to envisage
The human possibility.

R.P.W.: Certainly, I grant that, and
Who doesn't know down home
The intolerable eye of the sly one, and the sibilant
Confabulation below
The threshold of comprehension.

What the hell did you say?
Me, Boss? You mean me?
Who the hell you think I mean?
Me, Boss?

70

Yes, you—what the hell was that you said?
Boss, I did'n say nuthen.

Always nothing, but always something,
And in the deep vessel of your self now the dark
Dregs are disturbed, uncoil now, rise
To murk the rational ichor of innocence.
No use to say you've dealt justly with individuals
Or held the most advanced views on the race question.
Do you think the Dark Inquisitor can be deflected
By trivialities like that?

JEFFERSON: Do you think to instruct me?
I'd said there's no defense of the human definition.
And as for Lilburne, it's you who would seem
To defend him.

R.P.W.: No, I'd not defend him. No, not that,
But once we have him, no use to condemn a doom,
And I've got enough morbid curiosity
To want to know how Lilburne came to the hour
When stars sweat and the dear toad weeps in his hole.

But the word's not *know*. *Guess* will do better.
For even Lilburne couldn't *know*—knew only
The incredibleness of each deed done,
And unreality grew round him like a fog,
And he must strike through the fog, strike hard to find
Contact with something real,
Something that will, perhaps, scream out its reality,
And in that scream affirm, at last, poor Lilburne's own.
For all we all ask in the end is that:
Reality.

Or differently—how comic, really,
That one who yearns the most for love cannot
Bear to be loved, for love comes
Only as an accusation of guilt! So must
Destroy who loves to achieve at last
The secretly desiderated and ice-locked anguish

Of isolation.

Well, he's near done that now, Lilburne, I mean:
Mother and Father gone, Letitia sick
And still and white-lipped when he comes to her,
Aunt Cat with sulks and sulls and her deep grief.
The slaves all slow with hate like a disease,
And even the hound in the sweet midst of fawning
With a wary eye on Lilburne's right boot.

At least, so Lilburne thinks, and feels the twitch
Of nerve and muscle in the right leg.
He shoves the beast away. He doesn't want,
He honestly doesn't want, to kick the hound,
But the agonizing sweetness of possibility grows,
Grows now like love, so he yells:
"Fetch me the jug, John, damn it, fast!"
John comes, eyeballs sidewise, hand unsure,
And Lil stares at him till sweat runs out the kinks,
And in a whisper, vibrant as joy, whispers:
"You're sure one slow, ass-dragging, blue-gum bastard."

Then turns to Isham—

ISHAM: Yeah, yeah, he turned to me!
Me sitting there, and said: "I don't know why,
I just can't stand that slinking nigger bastard.
Looks like he just does something to me,
Something I just can't stand." So takes a drink.
And me, I don't say nothing.

R.P.W.: What's there to say?

ISHAM: And Lil, he looks at me like it's not me,
And says: "You just sit there, and nothing said."
And me: "Just nothing sort of came to say."
And him: "Whose side you on now, his or mine?"
And me: "Now, Lil, just listen—look here now—"
Then Lilburne: "Damn you, so you take his side."
And jumped up straight and hit the table hard.

72

"Oh, Lil!" I said. And sudden, he was gone.

R.P.W.: Up to his old tricks still. But tricks, no doubt,
He didn't invent. We've met those tricks before:
"Whose side you on?" Or: "You're against me, too."
There's nothing to wait for, then.

ISHAM: Yeah, he was mean sometimes, but that was Lil.
Not mean when I was little and we'd wrestle,
But later, once, when my strength was coming on,
I pestered him, and almost had him once, but he
Just squirmed like a cat, and grabbed
Me sly. No, not to throw—
To lift and fling me.
Then him just laughing,
Said: "You got to eat some more
Cornbread and buttermilk to be a man!"

I just lay there, my breath
All gone, and 'bout to cry.
Not from being hurt, but just he didn't
Love me, and Tishie ran toward me. He said:
"Don't touch the bugger, let him lie!
He'll learn."

And walked away.

"It's not he means to," our mother would say,
"It's just his blues come on. He loves you still."

But then—

R.P.W.: Then what?

ISHAM: Just I don't understand. Like the last—

R.P.W.: The last what?

ISHAM: Hell, it's no use to name the last thing now.
You got to tell it how it came on slow,

Then of a sudden there, like a gunshot—
Yeah, and Lilburne's face,
It keeps on staring, and my lips won't move
To say "Oh, Lil"—

But it's already happened.

Already, while far off,
Far off in the woods some son-of-a-bitch of a joree
Keeps singing his crazy son-of-a-bitch of a head off,
Like I didn't have a thing not better to do than listen
To that son-of-a-bitch of a bird sing his head off.

But there's no noise, not one, in the woods.
Every leaf hangs still, just that crazy bird,
And so I stand and Lilburne stares at me,
And maybe if I listen
To that son-of-a-bitch for just a second,
Then maybe nothing happened—but Lil—then Lilburne—
He falls.

R.P.W.: It was your own suggestion
To be more systematic, first things first,
And let whatever the deuce this last thing is
Go till the last. Suppose I summarize.
Well, to begin:
When Lucy's dead, things go from bad to worse.
Lilburne defends the spoons and civilization,
And beats the people.
Some pathological sadism provoked by him.
John gets the toughest. Lilburne can't stand him—
Yet John's his body-servant.
John tries the woods, comes back, gets beat again.
The drink gets worse—
And you're left alone with that brother you love so well.

ISHAM: But Lil—if you could know him, how he was—
A man and God-a-Mighty strong,
And laughed and rollicked when he wasn't blue,
"Old Ishey-Boy," he'd say, "Old Ishey-Boy"—

74

And the time he wrestled in the settlement—
You've seen a bear, how stout, well, that was Lil.
You've seen a bobcat, sly, well, that was Lil.
And a painter fast to jump, and jump again,
And it was Lil's face smiling
With teeth a-shine, then laughed out loud, and grabbed
That great big bully to heave him up sky-high.
You heard the crack on the ground.
Then folks all yelled.
Yelling Lil's name, and I said, marvel-slow,
So young I was—"Why, that's my brother there!"
'Twas like I prayed, me just a little bastard—
And asked the Lord to make me like my brother,
And make him love me, like I loved him then.

R.P.W.: Well, that was perfect preparation, sure,
And you were there, bound hand and foot, for Lilburne
To quarrel with, abuse, humiliate,
But never too much, always the right degree,
And always all, each act, in the name of love.
It's cat-and-mouse. He saves you for some stunned,
Truth-dazzled hour when the heart shall burst
In gouts of glory—hallelujah!—like a flower.
He awaits the hour of the Pentecostal intuition.

Knows it will come,

And so abides that beauty,
And therefore would merely reserve you
And plays with alienation.
Plucks you back,
Then draws you on,
Deeper and deeper in that darkling thicket
Of his dark dream,
And fades before you ever,
With sad face smiling and the beckoning hand,
With pity in the smile, and the lips soundlessly
Part to say,
"Oh, Ishey, little Ishey."
And fades before you. Goes. Now comes again,

75

And all the forest darker swells beyond,
And thorns, like guilt, will tear you as you plunge,
And cobwebs fetter you and fold your face
In terror of their weak tenacity.

Ah, deeper, deeper, has the dark no center?
Ah, deeper! has the night no moment poised
Before the stroke,
Where hope is happy and the dark hangs down
Like benediction and you smell the grass—
Remember how, in the dark, dew smells on the grass?—

Or was it like that?

ISHAM: There's just no way to reckon
How a thing happens to you.

R.P.W.: And summer passed, and sickness
Walked the land, and Nature creaked on its hinges
Like an old shed door at night when the wind shifts.
And the Terrible Year bloomed its malignancy,
The comet has come, and gone, dispensing its splendor.
And now December 15, 1811.
Do you recall exactly what happened that day?

ISHAM: Why, nothing—nothing happened—just a day.
But three days sooner, something happened then.
'Twas John, him back again from running off.

R.P.W.: I'd near forgot—yes, Lil beat John again.

ISHAM: But just a day,
Another day and dark a-settling down,
Like the world was tired,
So many years, and time, all passed away,
And fire on the hearth now low. You chunk it up.
Lil yelled for his jug.

R.P.W.: Let now the night descend
With all its graduated terrors,

And in its yearning toward absoluteness now amend
The impudent daylight's velleties, and errors,
For all life lifts and longs toward its own name,
And toward fulfillment in the singleness of definition.

So in the dark now let
The dark flame lift, unfolding like a flower
From the blind nutriment of Lilburne's heart—
That rich detritus of all History,
Muck, murk, and humus, and the human anguish,
And human hope.

Well, in this period of the final tumescence
From what fat oubliettes of inwardness
Let Lilburne speak.

What did he say, Isham?

ISHAM: He asked me did I really love our mother.

R.P.W.: And you, what did you say?

ISHAM: I said I loved her like always,
And once at night I dreamt she sang to me.
But, "Stop!" Lil yelled. And jumped up from his chair.
Then said: "Now what the hell made you tell that lie?"

But me: "It's true, she came. She came and sang.
She came and leaned like I was little and—"

And him: "A God-damned lie, you never dreamed it.
But me, I dream that dream, I guess I know.
She comes and smiles like years gone by
And I wait to hear her singing sweet and low—
But, oh—no sound, not ever a word, and her face,
It's dead—"

Then pushed his face up close:
"And don't you ever tell that lie again!"
And then so pitiful it hurt my heart:

"Oh, Ishey—Ishey—she never sings to me!"

And me: "But look—it's nothing but a dream."

And him: "She's dead, and black dirt chokes her singing.
But if you loved her—"

And me: "But, Lil—I do—"

And him, nigh whispering: "They steal her spoons."

And me: "But, Lil—"

He grabbed me by my shoulder:
"They tear the sheets where she lay down to die—
But you don't care—oh, you, you never loved her!"

And leans up close.

R.P.W.: Leans and the night
Grows big with possibility.
He knows that now is the time to know
If ever you, his Little Brother Isham,
Do truly love him and will take his hand.

ISHAM: Then points up to the shelf,
And says: "You see that pitcher there—
All gold and flowers, the one she loved so much
That the President, her brother, gave her
And she set up high to see."

I see the pitcher and I see his face.

"Listen," he says, "they're waiting now. They're waiting!"

There's nothing now to say. I see his eyes.

He took the pitcher down and stepped back quick.
"And you—oh, if you loved her—"
He holds the pitcher in his hands.

He's staring, jerks up his head, yells: "John!"

And John, he comes from the kitchen where he's squatting
Afore the fire, just snoozing like a nigger.
Comes footing slow.

Now things get queer. I never hated John.
Before, I mean. Him just another nigger.
But now to see him standing there so weak,
And frail to fall, and how his eyes were rolling,
It looked to me there wasn't a thing but hate
Inside me, and to hate that nigger John
For being so God-damn mean-weak was nothing
But sweet joy. And Lil
Was saying how he needed some fresh water
To mix his whiskey, and for John to go
Down to the spring and fetch it. Then I knew.
Then Lilburne was shoving the pitcher there to John.
I knew he would. John took it, and my breath
Came short. I just can't say:
"Look, John, don't take it!"

You see, I want him to.

And Lilburne's voice, far off, is saying:
"That is my mother's pitcher, and she loved it.
If anybody breaks my mother's pitcher—

I'll say no more.

Now, git!"

John moved off nigh the door. Then, "Wait!" says Lil,
And turns to me: "Now, Ishey,
Why don't you wake our people up and bring 'em
Up to the meat-house, make 'em make a fire.
We don't want folks come catching cold round here.
And let 'em sing, and maybe pat some juba.
Just pass the time till John and I get back."
    *

79

Then turns. Says "Ah." And down from the shelf,
He reaches for the pistol case,
And give 'em to me. "Now load," he says. "These niggers—
Just take these tricks, in case they get excited.
And me, I'll go with John. You see,
He's scared of the dark sometimes. But, John,
You're safe tonight. I'm right behind you.
I won't let Raw-Head scare pore little John."

They're gone, Lil soft behind,
And saying soft: "That pitcher—if you break it—"

R.P.W.: So you went down to the meat-house?

ISHAM: I roused our people out, all but Aunt Cat,
She's up at the big house, case of Tishie calling.
They built the fire, and got the meat-house ready.

R.P.W.: Ready for what?

ISHAM: For what?— If I'd just known—
And that's so God-durn queer,
How knowing and not knowing are the same,
And if what's going to happen
Will happen anyway, then what's the use—
But if I'd known—

R.P.W.: Well, there you go again,
Back on the old track, the desperate circle:
"If I'd known"—and the great Machine of History
Will mesh its gears sweetly in that lubrication
Of human regret, and the irreversible
Dialectic will proceed. That is, unless—
"If I had known!"—that is, unless we get
Some new and better definition of *knowing*.

ISHAM: Well, knowing—hell, it's just to know a thing,
Like anything you know—

R.P.W.: No, knowing can be,

Maybe, a kind of being, and if you know,
Can really know, a thing in all its fullness,
Then you are different, and maybe everything
Is different, somehow, too.

Oh, well, this won't help now,
For fire cracked high and made the chimney hum,
And light and shadow danced and swung together,
And your hands are sweating on the pistol butts,
And the people scrouge and hunker by the wall,
And you feel your own mouth moving, but can't hear
The words. And then—the door—

ISHAM: 'Twas John fell in.
Fell on his knees and elbows, like you'd shoved him.
But nobody shoved him, him just falling in,
Like somebody running and barely makes it.
Or somebody swimming out too far,
And suck or chute nigh gets him, and the sky
Swings high and the sun looks black and eyeballs bulging,
But he makes it in. He falls down on the ground.
So that nigger just fell in.

The pitcher-handle, he held it in his hand.

But the pitcher was gone. The pitcher wasn't there.

R.P.W.: Did that surprise you?

ISHAM: No, 'twas natural-like, and no surprise,
Like happened long ago.

R.P.W.: And John himself, no doubt, felt it as some
Peculiar fulfillment he had long lived with.

ISHAM: And the voice came from the dark outside.
'Twas like a voice that came from dark and air,
But it was Lilburne's face. It said: "Get in!"

So John crawled in. Lil shut the door.

"Now tie him up." Yeah, that was Lil.
Nobody moved. Not me, and not a nigger.
Lil said: "I give you niggers exactly one minute
To get that bastard tied." Two came and tied him.
John squinched eyes tight, lay nigger-mum.

Lil stepped across him, like he wasn't there.
And there was the meat-block there,
Nice tulip-wood, come from a whopping tree,
A section cross, and smooth to lay your hand.
Lil slapped his hand down. "Lay the bastard here."
And that fool nigger, he curled up little
To lie on that tulip-wood, his eyes squinched shut.

I reckon that fool nigger sort of figured
That what you never saw just couldn't be real,
So squinched his eyes. And Lilburne saying:
"Hand me that meat-axe, Ishey."

And me, I did.

The people moaned and hunkered to the wall.
And maybe that fool nigger never heard
What Lil was saying about spoons and sheets,
Nor heard him say: "But now's the last
Black son-of-a-bitching hand that ever,
So help me God, will make my mother grieve!"

The axe came down, Lil flung the hands in the fire.

JEFFERSON: Enough! We know the rest.

ISHAM: And the axe
Came down, and whacked his feet that ran away.
Lil flung 'em into the fire,
And the axe—

R.P.W.: All right, we know the whole preposterous
Butchery. But one thing more:
Did John cry out at the last?
          *

ISHAM: Yeah, that fool nigger spread his mouth to yell.
You got to yell if ever they start chopping.
But me, I ne'er heard—
Like all that nigger could yell was just a hunk
Of silence—you don't even hear it when the meat-axe
Gets in, gets through, goes *chunk*, chunks on the wood.
It's funny how that *chunk* just won't come clear.
Yeah, the axe comes down,
But not a sound, and that nigger spreads his mouth,
And I strain and strive
To hear—oh, Lord, if only—
Then maybe something gets finished.

Or maybe it's not real, since I can't hear—
But I know—

JEFFERSON: Oh, it is the only real thing.
We are born to joy that joy may become pain.
We are born to hope that hope may become pain.
We are born to love that love may become pain.
We are born to pain that from that inexhaustible superflux
We may give others pain—

MERIWETHER: Yes, we are born to—

ISHAM: And when that nigger spreads his mouth so wide—

JEFFERSON: Oh, what's one nigger more
In the economy of pain?
And Lilburne—what's one more
Bloody and sentimental maniac?
Or you, Isham, trapped and stupid—
What's one more corruptible simpleton?
Or those people hunched by the wall—
Oh, yes, they moaned, but don't forget they tied him.

I am talking about the texture in which
One episode of anguish evokes all anguish
And sets nerves screaming and white tendrils curl
In black peripheries beyond the last stars, and—

*

83

R.P.W.: If I am informed on the facts,
Though you could not, apparently, bring yourself to speak
Of the family scandal, you continued, to declare,
In general terms of course, your old faith
In man and made the boast
Cut in the stone, on your mountain in Albemarle.

JEFFERSON: One thing: when old it is hard to deprive others
Of hope. And hard, when old, to surrender
What you had taken to be the significance of life.
My hope died hard. I confess
That at the first information
There was merely the shock, for I had not yet surmised
How hope but feeds on hope, and in the cat's cradle
We weave and call our life and philosophy,
There's that single strand that, if plucked—and in
The card-castle, the single card—no, it
Was not like that.
No, despite the violence of the first shock
There was no
Immediate impairment of the general structure of
My hope. Even when I shuddered for the future
Of our country, I would say of my own plight,
This is merely a personal anguish.

R.P.W.: Lilburne was kin, that's true, but grown now,
Not now what you once called the sweet parcel of flesh
On a pillow. Blood thins with age and distance. So
Your anguish seems, at least, excessive.

JEFFERSON: But by what standard excessive? I had no son.
Yes, Meriwether had been a sort of son,
And I saw him an image of
The straight-backed and level-eyed men to come,
Worthy of the gleaming miles of our distance.
But he was dead. Dead,
They told me, by his own hand, in Tennessee, and I wept.

MERIWETHER: Spare your tears!
    *

84

JEFFERSON: But there were my sister's sons, the sister who
Had lived, somehow, all the years in my imagination—
Gentle by cradle and hearthside,
And I felt a pang of sweetness at what had been long denied me.
I controlled the pang. There was always contrivance
And the larger hope.
She left her sons, and I said that they, far away,
By swale or inimical forest,
Would fulfill her, and my heart.
You know the rest.

But I could not accept it. I tried
To buckle the heart past fondness or failure.
But the pain persisted, and the encroachment of horror.
I saw the smile of friendship as a grimace of calculation.
I saw the victuals on my plate in their undeclared context,
Mucous of oyster, beard of mussel, harslet of hog,
And even the choice viand as a shadow of ordure.
My eyes would wander from the instructive page,
And my heart crunched like a chick in the sow's jaw.

I said, I must cling more sternly to the rational hope.

Well, when in privacy of pain I died, I let
The old epitaph be put on stone. But only
Because I had no right to rob
Man of what hope he had. And what's
One more lie in the tissue of lies we live by?
But long since
The axe had been set at the root of hope,
And as history divulged itself,
I saw how the episode in the meat-house
Would bloom in Time, and bloom in the lash-bite
And the child's last cry, down in the quarters when
The mother's sold. And for another joke,
Ask the Christian Cherokee
How the heart bled westward on the Trail of Tears.

R.P.W.: Well, speaking of Indians, the Smithland courthouse
Has one nice record, how on Saturday night

In Eddyville, down in the tavern there,
Some heroes of our national destiny
Kicked an old Chickasaw to death, for sport.
And a slave—

JEFFERSON: And for another joke, I've seen
How vanity, greed, and blood-lust may obscenely
Twine in the excuse of moral ardor and crusade.
Yes, that's your funniest!
Oh, it's always the same,
And the dust drinks blood—
And Bloody Angle and the Bloody Pond—
Or listen, flames crackle through the Wilderness
And the green briar burning smells like myrrh, but that other
More pungent odor is not myrrh, the odor
That so reminds you of the odor in the meat-house.
The wounded scream. Then cease. The flame has found them.

Well, let them scream. All's one in the common collusion.

But a few more items from the ample documentation—
Pittsburgh and Pinkerton and the Polack bleeding
In some blind alley, while the snow falls slow,
And Haymarket, Detroit and Henry's goons—
Oh, that's enough—and how much since!
And Boston sleeps and Philadelphia, too,
And sleep is easy over the starlit continent I once loved,
For all is safe now, and the stars hold their
Accustomed formations. Take your screw. And sleep.
If you can sleep. If you
Can no longer hear the scream from the meat-house.

ISHAM: That nigger spreads his mouth, but I swear to God
I can't hear nothing—

JEFFERSON: Well, you're lucky, then.

ISHAM: But that's the trouble, looks like could I just
One time just hear that yell, then I could sleep.
            *

JEFFERSON: Oh, what's
One nigger more or less—except he's all,
And all responsibility now spreads.
It spreads like a stain in water, and—

R.P.W.: Well,
If you would speak of responsibility,
There's the not unfashionable notion to consider
That John himself was in a strange way responsible.

JEFFERSON: Oh, yes, the pitcher—my miserable pitcher.

R.P.W.: Only because he wanted, in the end,
To curl on the meat-block, draw his knees up little,
And squinch his eyes and know the expectant deliciousness
Before the axe fell—oh, yes, you've seen how,
When reapers ring round the last of the standing grain,
The rabbit runs to the stone hurled by the boy's hand,
And the stone's parabola and the rabbit's irrational
Skitter fulfill each other, and that fulfillment
Is a chord of music big enough
To blacken the sky.
And the hen in the dark henhouse offers her throat
To the delicate stitch of the weasel's tooth and to the lip's
Insidious suction, and with one muted squawk, automatic,
Surrenders to that saccharine surgery—and with the prurience
Of morning you've seen in the henhouse the blowzy
Victim askew, like an overnourished matron on the divan,
Out-thrust and disordered, the eyes filmed over, hands lax,
After the hired lover has taken his exit.

JEFFERSON: So you'd make what you call masochism the final obscenity?
And after that obscenity nothing—

R.P.W.: No, don't blame me, I just report a notion.
The victim
Becomes the essential accomplice, *provocateur*—
No, more, is the principal. And the real victim
Is he whose hand was fatally elected to give the stroke,
But is innocent. So the line of the old poem,

See where the Victor-victim bleeds, takes on
A new significance,
And John trembles with sweetness at Lilburne's gaze.

Poor Lilburne—how could he escape?

JEFFERSON: Stop!
If there is truth in what you say—and yes,
There's truth, but a truth the heel would slew in
As it slews in ordure in the dark alley—
But it's still a truth
That extenuates nothing, and for you to make
Lilburne the victim is only—

R.P.W.: Oh, that's not it.
I only nag the question. And if Lilburne
Is John's victim, it's only a manner of speaking—
A way to say we're all each other's victim.
Potentially, at least.

JEFFERSON: What does that prove?
What does anything prove in the face of the naked scream?

R.P.W.: Nothing.
For there's no gold the acid of anguish
Will not, in the end, eat. And the axe fell.
And when there was no sound,
Shall we suppose, but Lilburne's labored breath,
What remained on the block was heaved in the fire,
And the hot coals hissed, flame sagged, jerked blue and white,
Then settled dutifully to the new task,
And to the sound of that protracted sizzle
The prayers resumed by the wall. When all had burned—
That is, all that would burn—Lilburne said—

ISHAM: He turned from the fire, the people hunkered.
His face a-shining where the sweat had popped.
And said: "You niggers stop that racket.
Or if you've got to pray, you better pray
God'll help keep count on my mother's spoons.

You've seen that nigger John. Well, now you know."

They get up quiet and soft-foot long the wall.

He turned again, like something he'd forgot.
He called two back. They stood and sweated.
"Get those damned bones," he said, "and dig a hole."
No big hole 'twas. They dumped the durn bones in.
The niggers left. Then Lil, he stomped and smoothed.

Then like a breath, I thought how quiet it was.
The moon so bright, a-coming clear for frost.
"It's coming frost," I said, like nothing happened.
It felt so natural, tears came in my eyes.
It felt so natural, like I loved the world,
And trees and stars and rocks and everything—
They leaned and loved me, too.
But then—

R.P.W.: But then, no doubt, the earthquake?

ISHAM: Yeah, yeah, just when my heart went big and sweet,
It hit. I hit the ground.

R.P.W.: Well, the folk version says you moaned and prayed
And called on God for mercy. But Lilburne,
He danced on the ground that shook like jelly,
And cackled to the moon, and yelled:
"Don't call on God, He'd spit you in the face!
Call on the Devil, for he loves us both!"

ISHAM: Oh, no—it didn't come like that.

R.P.W.: I never thought so. You see, that version
Would violate Lilburne's deepest character.
We know that Lilburne's not the Devil's son,
Even if the warrant that they swore for him does say
That Lilburne Lewis, *gentleman*,
Not having fear of God before his eyes,
But being moved and seduced by the instigation

89

Of the Devil, thus did his so-and-so.

No, Lilburne had no truck with the Evil One,
But knew that all he did was done
For his mother and the sweetness of the heart—

JEFFERSON: But not the less evil therefor,
Or for whatever mask or smirk may be devised,
And if evil is all—

R.P.W.: Who said it was? I didn't.
For we might say that Lilburne's heart-deep need
To name his evil good is the final evidence
For the existence of good.

JEFFERSON: And if that's all,
Why not say evil is evil, and not sweeten
Your slobber with any pap of paradox?

R.P.W.: I know how trivial you find
My present argument. But anyway,
When earth shook and oak trees moaned like men
And the river sloshed like dish-suds in a pan,
Poor Lilburne didn't name the Devil's name.

ISHAM: He fell down too, like me. I lay on the ground.
I lay and all my belly churned to die.
I saw the moon spin round, and light get green.
I knew the End of Time. And it came to me so awful
How a minute back I saw the moon all clear,
But earth—it shook and threw me down. But I ne'er prayed.

What's there to pray for if the sweet thing comes
Too late and slow, and goes, and leaves you lay?
Why don't it come a time when it can stay?
Why don't it come before the awful happened?
A half a minute sweet, then the earth—
It shakes, it throws you down.

R.P.W.: Yes, God shook out the country like a rug,

And sloshed the Mississippi for a kind of warning—
Well, if God did, why should he happen to pick out
Just Lilburne's meanness as excuse? There'd been God's plenty
Of such excuses, and they multiply
Right now in Old Kaintuck, without any earthquakes
Nor Year of Wonders
To scare the homefolks with appropriate omens,
As when, nightlong, the statue of Hercules
In the Forum sweated, and Commodus ate dung.

There was an earthquake, sure. But you got up,
And lived, somehow.

ISHAM: The way folks live,
And every breath you draw or gobbet chew
Just goes to say that nothing, nothing, ever happened.

R.P.W.: Yes, say that life, after all, is possible
Only because of the discontinuity
Of life—not life in a lump, your fate or definition.
So Isham lives, and night by night with Lilburne sits.

The mother's dead, the father gone, bones buried,
Letitia gone, with the scream yet filling her head.

LETITIA: It filled my head, but I hung on
And rode. I made the settlement. They took me down.
My brother came, but when I tried
To explain things, the words,
They came all wrong—

BROTHER: They sure did.
You gabbled like a guinea hen, and it was a skunk
Sucking her clutch of eggs, and never let on
How I had me a ground
To cut the bastard's heart out. Yeah,
You made me a fool to ride to Rocky Hill,
And me not knowing, and him as sweet as pie,
And called me "Brother," and that nigger—
Cat's her name—I never liked her,

Too God-damned sly, saying "Yassuh, yassuh,"
And bows and bobs,
And her too clean to be a nigger, noway.

Lil called her in.
"Now tell how 'twas," he said, "how Miss Tishie left."
"Earthquake," was what she said, "and she got notions
Somebody yelled, and kept on yelling."
Then Lilburne stopped her: "Cat, did you hear something?"
She squinched her eyes right slow, then ast:
"Now what you ast me, Mr. Lil, my Honey?"

And ain't no nigger gonna call me Honey.

Then Lilburne: "You better listen better.
I said, did you hear yelling here last night?"
"Why, Chile," she said, and squinched her eyes,
"Whatever 'twas I heard, you heared it too."
"Damn it," says Lilburne, "try and recollect,
And tell the gentleman how Poor Miss Tishie
Gets things mixed up. But you—did you hear something?"

And Cat says: "Lawd!—oh, Lawd, I hears it yet,
And turble wild it comes, and comes—"
"God-damn," says Lilburne, and his face went white.
And I said: "Lilburne, I'd just like to know
Whatever the hell it was yore nigger did hear."

"The owl," she said, "he scritch. And scritch agin."
And me: "If a scritch-owl scritch,
Now who the hell cares? Let the bastard scritch."
"He scritch agin," she said, "and then hit come!"

"What came?" said Lilburne, sharp. He grabbed her arm.

"Honey," she said, all gentle-like, "why, Honey,
Not nuthen. Jist the ole yearth-quake."

R.P.W.: So Cat now tortured Lilburne for her sport,
Just teetered on the verge of revelation,

Then caught her balance: "Jist the old yearth-quake."
No, not a sport. It isn't exactly that.
She would set the scene for poor Letitia's tale,
Not tell it herself, for Lilburne was her Honey—
Deny Letitia's tale, but in denial
Declare the truth—

BROTHER: She did'n declare nuthen, that fool nigger, jist says:
"Ain't nothen happened here at Rocky Hill.
Not here at Rocky Hill. We loves one t'other."

And Lilburne said: "Get out." And out she got.

He looked round then at me, and said: "Dear Brother,
You've heard the nigger tell what happened here.
A chimney fell, the river roared—that's all.
It scared your sister, my beloved wife,
But when she's ready to come back, you tell her
The door is open wide, and my arms, too,
And my heart will break with her society gone."
He talked so fine, just like he was a preacher,
And shook my hand, and slapped me on the shoulder,
And poured me likker, and I drank it down.

Yeah you—you, Tishie—you made a fool of me!

R.P.W.: Well, gabble got the gossip started,
And sent the Sheriff. A sort of social call,
The bumpkin overawed
By Lewis greatness and old Jefferson.
He says he's heard they had some nigger trouble.
And Lilburne: "Yes, that nigger John.
You know how niggers are, you get one ornery,
One thing to do. So he high-tailed for the woods."

He shrugs: "And I hope he don't come back."
That shrug's impressive to the frontier Sheriff,
Five hundred dollars gone, and a Lewis shrugs.

The slaves don't talk.
        *

And life goes on at Rocky Hill, goes on,
Enters a phase of stillness,
And Lilburne's soul lolls in his breast, lapt
In a dark, luxurious satiety.
It stretches its kingly members in shadowy, somnolent ease,
And we think of eyes that close,
And unclose, with muted glitter in
That indolence of dark.

V

R.P.W.: So night after night, the two,
Ringed by the continent that breathes in darkness,
Sit. No cups
Are broken now. No spoons are lost.
There is order in the house and all the appurtenances
Of civilization are defended.
The portraits stare from the walls, in approbation.
The house has been set on the headland, on stone, against
The disorder of the wild land.
Lilburne would defend civilization, define
The human mission, bring light to the dark place.
But what does he defend?

Only a pitcher, poor symbol.

Does Lilburne know all this?
He does not know.

The winter wanes.
Time is divulged, and the earth
Yet shakes, but men accommodate
The heart to the horror.

Why not? Long ago,
They had accommodated themselves to being men,
And the work of the world goes on.

The red-bud shall order forth its flame at the incitement of sun.
The maple shall offer its golden wings for the incitement of air.
Powder of oak-bloom shall prank golden the deerskin shirt
Of the woodsman, like fable. Gleaming and wind-tossed, the raw
Conclamation of crows shall exult from the swale-edge.
The redbird whistles, the flame wing weaves,
And the fox barks in the thicket with its sneezing excitement.
The ceremony of joy is validated in the night cry,

And all earth breathes its idiot and promiscuous promise:
Joy.

But Lilburne walks not forth.
His face will not be seen in sun
Or leaf-pattern of shadow.
His heart does not unlatch when the first shoots
Of corn prick punctiliously the black field,
For he now inhabits an inward landscape
Of forms fixed and hieratic, like moon-blasted basalt.

But Lilburne is gentle now with Little Ishey—
That strong young brute that wears the gentle face.
And gentle with the people of the house.
He can be gentle now because he knows
The time draws on.

The man comes down the trace.
Sees the hound, the Sheriff gets the bone.
It's human, fire-black, and some shred of flesh
Yet clings where flame or hound-tongue had failed in duty.
The bone is scarcely evidence, but we guess
How far the gossip's gone if this can make
The Sheriff jam his hat on, yell for his horse.
For we can guess how in the web of grievous
Suspicion sick Letitia's gabble wove,
The Sheriff's own name threaded with the warp.

We hear the voices: "*Yeah, the bastard's skeered.*"
The voices: "*Yeah, he'd lick a Lewis' spit.*"
The voices: "*Yeah, I bet he taken his'n.*"
He hears the voices, hears them in his head.
And so leaps up.

ISHAM: "Look! here they come," say I, "him and his men a-riding,"
And Lil, he watched, and in a whisper-like:
"The Sheriff." I figured he was scared.
But he's not scared. Not Lil. His eyes are shining.

"Well, gentlemen," he called out, fair and hearty,

"Get down, I'm proud you've come." They get down slow.
"And, Sheriff," Lil said, "take a drink and honor me!"
He hummed and hawed, the Sheriff.
Then squared off sharp:
"Well, Mr. Lewis, I'll say much obliged
For yore good likker, but I'm here for duty.
I pray you, sir, to call yore niggers up."
And Lil just smiled: "Why, Sheriff, sure.
My house is yours, poor thing though it may be."
The Sheriff then: "They ain't a damn thing wrong
With yore big house. You take me fer a fool?"
But Lil, he smiled and said, nigh whispering:
"Why, Sheriff, that's merely a way of speaking
To be polite. For who might recognize the fact."
"God-damn," the Sheriff said, and flushed up black.
He chewed his mad. Then quiet: "I want them niggers."
And Lil: "Why, Sheriff, sure. Yes, Ishey, call 'em."

I got the niggers. They stood there.
The Sheriff pulled a parcel out his pocket,
Wrapped in a rag, his handkerchief, I guess.
He gave it to Lilburne. "Look at that," he said.
And Lil unwrapped it, slow. It was a bone.
It was a jawbone, man's, and black from fire.

"You know that bone?" I heard the Sheriff saying.
And Lilburne say: "A bone's a bone, and, Sheriff,
If you believe you have a duty here,
Then do it. And get gone. I've else to do
Than handle all the offal you drag in."

And dropped the bone.

The Sheriff picked it up.

He swung to the niggers, held it high:
"This is a nigger's bone, and you know who.
I am the Law! I want them bones.
Show me them bones—and if you don't, you're nuthen
But a coward passel of niggers! Who's a man?"
        *

He stood and waited. Lil just smiled.
A catbird whistled once, but never a word.

And Lilburne smiles, and said: "You see."

If Lil said nothing, maybe till this day
Those niggers might just stood all sull and mum.
But Lil, he laughed: "A passel of niggers, ha!"

Then turned, and spat.

And then it happens, comes a voice so high
All old and screechy, like some old scritch-owl,
"Bones will fly up!" it scritches. "Bones will rise.
I see them bones, they're flyin' to the sky!"

It was Aunt Cat. She fell down on the ground,
A-staring in the sky, like bones was flying.

Then niggers yelling so, and gabbling wild.
"Them bones!" they yelled, and pointed to the sky.
And one—one of the blue-gums what had tied up John—
He ran to the Sheriff, fell down to grab his knees.
"Oh, Lawd," he yelled, "oh, Valley—oh, Jehoshaphat!
Oh, white folks, save me, I'll show them bones."

R.P.W.: So that was it. Aunt Cat again.
Not that she did it—she would not betray
Her Honey-Chile she once had given suck to.
Nor show the bones, just see them in the sky.

But why right then? What made her seize that moment?
An easy guess: it was that Lilburne spat.
Remember how, long back, when the mother dies
And Cat says how she'd given suck
And was his Mammy too—then Lilburne spat.
Spat out her milk, and all her niggerness.
So again he trips the latch of the old anguish,
And nigger bones fly up to kiss the sky.
Oh, it's no trick—she sees them, literally,

98

And utters her screech of glory and anguish and then
Collapses. And knows her Honey-Chile
Is gone forever, so shuts her eyes,
Lies there and lets the human confusion
Blow past, blow past like dead leaves whirled.

The white folks go. The black folks tote her in.

ISHAM: They dug the bones and put 'em in a sack.
"Now, Mr. Lewis," the Sheriff said,
"If it's yore pleasure now, we'll be a-riden."
"It is my pleasure, sir," Lil said, and laughed.

And so we rode, him humming all the way.
'Twas "Barby Allen" that he hummed.

R.P.W.: Did he already have the end in mind?
No, I'd reckon not. Just had
The certainty of moving toward
That perfect certainty of self that all
His life had yearned for. The cliff trees
Keep the track of the old blast, and the only
Knowledge worth the knowing is
The knowledge too deep for knowing.

So Lilburne took his certainty to town.
Found guarantors to make his bond.
We know their names, Rogers, Bolen, Dyer,
Cannon, and Hollinshead, all good names yet,
Good householders of that dark vicinage.

And so back home. Back home to wait.
For what, from the Grand Jury, would come:

Lilburne Lewis, he with an axe
Of the value of two dollars ($2.00)
Held in his hands, did willfully and maliciously
And with hate, cut a death wound—

Meanwhile, Time turns, and the orbed axis leans

To warm Kentucky closer to the sun,
To sprig the black earth with the corn's bright blade
Among the black boles fire had left to rot.
But there is forest yet, and buds are bursting,
And morning's march wakes birdsong mile by mile,
One drowsy note in green gloom, then the glory.
Song washes westward through the wilderness.
The dawn lifts westward, and the dogwood bursts.

This is the hour of Lilburne's sleep, the hour
When dream turns inward, groping for the heart.
His dream now finds the heart. It takes its ease,
And that poor body sprawls on the tumbled bed.
In dawn the swart face now is streaked with pale.
One arm is flung to the bed's emptiness,
And the faint odor of vomit would assail the nostrils.

Waking, he will, no doubt, be seized as ever
By a momentary incredulity,
And think: "But it's not me—oh, no, not me!"
Then know. But before the glacial acceptance, cry,
Just once, to the empty room: "God!"

Then know, and be, himself.

Joy flickers, shy, in the heart's
Cold fatigue. But joy is energy.
There is one germ for joy. Its name is vision.
The scales are loosed from his eyes.

So sits, with Isham, by the hearth, now cold, and feels
The April night grow big. And darkness
Peers in through the open door.
The annual fragrance now, like memory, swells
In darkness to seduce the heavy sense,
And peepers, far off, with their insidious monotone,
Prick night, and from some star-stung dingle
The whippoorwill offers his heartbroken comment.

It comes here faint, but with veracity.
          *

100

Ah, man must love his own necessity.
But it is hard to find, so hard and slow.
The last phase: the threshold of recognition.
The last phase: the kiss of necessity.
The last phase: the self fades into fate.

ISHAM: We'd sit inside, the candle sagging,
But Lil kept writing, like he did a-night now.
He'd lean and study, the gray-goose-quill gone still.
Then write, so slow to make it fair.

One night I asked, and he snapped short at me.
"Business," he says, "and business not for boys."

Then I looked out the window.
The river's black. Some stars, they shine in it.
Then music, far away.
I felt like crying. Like a sprig. For lonesomeness.
Then: "Lil!" I say. He never budged.
And music closer now. I hear a fiddle.

Then see the light, down river-blackness sliding.
A keelboat sliding down, I bet, and a fire on it,
And far off, folks a-singing, and the words
Not clear, then clearer, coming down the dark:

> Sliding down the river,
>   Lean on the beechen oar,
> All the way to Shawneetown,
>   Long time ago.

Then me to Lil: "Oh, can't you hear?"
But Lil: "Shut up." And me:
"Folks going somewhere. Somewhere they got to go!"

Go singing down the darkness while my eyes get wet.

Then through the window, like the stillest breath,
It came a-sudden from the dark outside
A big green moth, so big you'd never see,
The palest green like some ghost leaf alive,

101

Blown on a breeze you couldn't feel,
Nor brush your cheek with cool. And that big moth,
It came so ghost-green by
And settled on the paper, nigh to Lil.
Lil looked at it.

Then lifted up his hand—oh, slow.

The moth, it moved its wings, so quiet and slow,
Lil staring at it. His hand rose, slow.

I saw it rising there. The hand, I mean, and knew
That if it came down like it could,
The fingers crook'd out wide, and fast like a painter's paw,
Then that would be
The end of something. God-durn, I couldn't say
Just what.

One second, then, as cold as ice,
I hated Lil.

And that was terrible
To hate your brother. I sweated cold.

The hand was high as it could go.

I shut my eyes, then opened 'em, and what I saw—
The hand was coming slow, and not to scare.
It touched the tabletop a-nigh, but gentle-still.

My breath came back.

Then, slow as a dream, that green thing moved.
But ne'er a wing, a-creeping slow.
It clomb Lil's finger, the finger
Ne'er moving. The thing clomb up.
There, there, the wings
So gentle fanned, and frail
But not to fly, but like it had a mind
To spread and make a show for folks to see.

Then gentle, gentle, Lil's hand rose, the moth on his finger still.
He reached so high, then stopped. It didn't scare.
Not scared, but slow, it drifted off his finger, high.
The wings ne'er moved, to fan and fly,
Just drifting off just like the time had come
To go where it would go, and say goodbye.
The thing was gone in the dark outside our door.

Lil watched the empty air.

Then brisk, he turned to me:
"You asked me what I wrote, Old Ishey-Boy,"
He said, and smiled like him, my sweetest brother.
"Well," he said, "read it," and shoved the paper at me:

In the name of God Amen This my last will—

I saw the words. My guts went cold.
"Why, it's your will," I said. He grinned.
"You make your will," he said, "when the time draws on."
"But, Lil—" I said.

"And the time draws on," he said.

"But, Lil—" I said, and my breath got choked,
Like nights when the nightmare came and I'd wake up
And feel my throat, then know it was a dream.
"Oh, you're afraid they'll hang us," I heard him say
Like he would name my dream. Then grinned:
"Well, Ishey-Boy, we sort of killed the nigger!"
And me: "But just a nigger"—and my breath got choked—
"Just a nigger you said had done our mother wrong!"

He slapped my knee. "Forget it, son," he said,
"I'll never let 'em hang my Ishey-Boy."
Then sharp: "Read on."

And I read on about his business,
And how he left our father his fine horse,
The one he bought from Hurley, with the blaze,

And his rifle-gun, shot-bag, and walking stick,
And the hound-dog Nero he loved so well.
And named Letitia beloved but cruel.
I threw it down.
The words, they looked so queer.

He picked it up. "Read on," he said. I read.
Within this inclosure myself and my brother requests
Be entered in the same coffin and
In the same ground.

But *ground* scratched out, and then
'Twas *grave* he writ. I read the words.
Then of a sudden saw the sense, and all.
Saw *brother* writ. And knew the word was me.

'Twas me, 'twas Isham, in the ground and grave.
And called out: "Lil—it's me that's here!"
And he, right soft: "Why, Ishey, yes, it's you."
"But, Lil," I said, "you said just now they wouldn't—"
"Oh, Ishey-Boy," he said, "oh, you can trust me."
"But, Lil—" I said—

And he: "Oh, Ishey—not alone."
"But dead!" I cried.

He kicked his chair back, jumped and spat.
"What's to be dead!" he said.
"You can be dead,
And breathe and eat and sleep
And purge your gut and walk inside your clothes."
Then pointed: "Oh, see the folks all walking in their clothes!"

He stared like folks was there, but I couldn't see 'em:
"Don't know they're dead and stinking in their clothes!"

"But, Lil," I said, "it ain't us dead!—
For listen, we'll up and ride,
Get saddled up and gone and fast and far.
Tonight, to Mississippi or what they name the Arkansas,

Or West, like Cousin Meriwether went
To spy the land, out where folks' foot would come.
Where mountains are big and where the ocean is.
Oh, it's a country wide and parlous big
And fair to be, like 'twas a new world come!"

"The world!" he said. And spat: "It's all the same!
Where'er you go the world all stinks the same."

And me: "But, Lil—we'd be alive!"

His face went naked: "Yes, you'd ride!
Just up and ride and leave our mother here."
"But, Lil, she's dead!"
And him: "She loves you still,
But you don't love her—no, you're scared of rope!"

He grabbed his neck, and let his tongue stick out
Like he was hanging. But a-sudden, laughed:
"Oh, Ishey, I'll not let them hang my boy.
They'll never string up Ishey like a cat,
Not my Old Ishey up to kick and squirm
And wet his pants while all the folks are laughing.
Oh, no!"

And lower leaned, and held me close,
Like he would love me. Then broke out laughing,
And tickled me like times long back
When we were children playing on the floor,
And I laughed, too, like nothing's happened.
We rolled and laughed there on the floor.
Like we were little and no time gone by.

Then all was still, him in a chair, my head
Propped by his knee. My head
Felt heavy, like sleep coming on.
His hand was lying on my head like he loved me.

R.P.W.: So had you there at last. Yes, all was his.
Now he could sit till dawn. His soul was still.

⁜

ISHAM: Yeah, yeah, we sat while light came slow,
And the candle died before the day had come.
Then gray came in the window and the door.
The hound went to the door and smelled the air.
The hound came back, licked Lilburne's hand.

So Lil got up and slapped me on the shoulder,
Said: "Ishey, it's today.
Oh, Ishey-Boy, we go a journey soon."
Then put his papers in his pocket
That they would be there when the time came on.

R.P.W.: To face each other over your mother's grave?

ISHAM: Yeah, Lil would count to ten.

R.P.W.: Why not count three?—No, that would be too quick!
Lil couldn't watch you then, and relish all
That all his time had groaned for, hour by hour.

ISHAM: What made him count so slow, and stare?

R.P.W.: To get the last sweet drop. But tough luck, Lil.
Just as you face each other at the grave,
You shoot yourself by accident, and so
The curtain's down before the show begins.

ISHAM: But listen here—

R.P.W.: To what?

ISHAM: To how it was. It never came like that.

R.P.W.: Why not? After they'd caught you, and
On April 11, John Darrah, he being coroner,
Called in his jury, and you
Made deposition, swearing that
Lilburne in trying an experiment
Accidentally shot himself dead—
And they believed you, for the charge to you

Reads not for murder, just accessory
To Lilburne's death—

ISHAM: But it wasn't true. Not what I swore.

R.P.W.: Well, what?

ISHAM: Lil stood up there and counted slow,
And staring steady at me all the time.
To stare and count—
Count *four*, count *five*—

No, not my Lil!

MERIWETHER: Oh, yes, it is!

LILBURNE: Six!

ISHAM: And yonder, off in the woods a joree's calling—

LILBURNE: Seven!

ISHAM: And yonder, off in the woods, every leaf—

LILBURNE: Eight!

ISHAM: —is still, but the son-a-bitch of a bird—
Oh, Lil—oh, make him stop!

LILBURNE: Nine!

ISHAM: —and I thought, if only that
Son-of-a-bitch—

Then I stand there and see my pistol.
The smoke hangs blue at the muzzle, like I'm dreaming,
And my voice, it yelled: "Oh, Lil, I never meant to!"

But him on the ground—and the blood.
                *

R.P.W.: Well, what a fool! I see it all!
How Lilburne counted slow to make you do it,
He knew you'd crack, and be
His last betrayer, and leave him in his perfectest delight,
Alone, alone, in that sweet alienation, yes, sucking
That sweet injustice like a Christmas bonbon.

And don't you see how as a corollary
Because you loved him, he betrayed you, too?
Betrayed you when he made you murder him,
And broke his solemn promise—
"Oh, Ishey-Boy, I'll never let you hang!"

ISHAM: I could a-shot myself—I could a-done it—

R.P.W.: But Lilburne knew you never would—yes, knew
You well, and knew you'd break and run.

ISHAM: I don't—know—nothing.
But yeah, I lied—because I didn't want folks thinking
I killed my brother, when I loved him so.

R.P.W.: Why not admit you hated him?

LUCY: No! No!—for if you loved him once
That love is valid yet and all you have
To bring with you into the inhabited darkness.

JEFFERSON: I would have done it with my own hands!

MERIWETHER: Yes, Jeff, less slyly than to me.

JEFFERSON: Who are you, Crack-Head?

R.P.W.: My God!—it's Meriwether!

ISHAM: Got his soldier hat off, yeah! —Got it in his hand,
And you can see! See the big busted hole in his head!
And he grins, he points—
    *

R.P.W.: The brains stare out like one great eye,
Winking in blood—

MERIWETHER: Oh, yes, the brains, they stare
In absolute knowledge. And if—

ISHAM: Look—he's laughing!

MERIWETHER: And if I'm Crack-Head now, Old Jeff,
You ought to recognize your handiwork.

JEFFERSON: My handiwork?

MERIWETHER: I was that fool fish to which
Your lie was the perfect lure. Oh, sure, I gulped
It down—your nobleness.

JEFFERSON: Oh, son—

MERIWETHER: Son for one instant, once. Then—

JEFFERSON: I see—I see the old mark of your pain.
But I never contrived for else than your good.
As I understood it, and what miscarriage
Came toward that desperate dawn in Tennessee
When you groped the gourd in the dry bucket
For water—water—and the sad moon
Westward sagged, and nobody came—
It's not my doing, no! And I wept to hear.
You'll not say I—

MERIWETHER: I'll say the truth, for if
I lived the lie you taught me, I died
A truth. I cracked my head
And let the lie fly wide. —Look!
It's gone. Look in the hole—
Just the bloody pulp that is truth.

JEFFERSON: Oh, Meriwether!

*

MERIWETHER: Yes!—and murdered by your lie.
It was your lie that sent me forth, in hope,
To the wilderness—

JEFFERSON: If it was ease you sought—

MERIWETHER: You know why I went forth.
And with your letter in my pocket,
The letter writ the Day of Liberty,
July 4, 1803. It said:
And to give more entire satisfaction & confidence
To those who may be disposed to aid you,
I Thomas Jefferson, President
Of the United States of America, have written
This letter of general credit for you
With my own hand and signed it with my name.
  TH: Jefferson.

But could that save me?

So went forth.

I and my dear friend Clark, and forty-three men—
Soldiers, French watermen, the tough Kentuckians,
And my good nigger York, who left his seed
In every tribe across the continent.
And bales of junk to please the savages,
Breechclouts and scarlet cloth and burning glasses,
Red leggings, blankets, medals, and ear-wire.
The month was May. We set sail
In the late afternoon breeze, camped on the first island.
And so entered upon my life.
My death.

Entered the land where the sky lifts west, like wings.
We entered the land of the enormousness of air.
For a year we moved toward the land
Of the Shining Mountains.

That is their name.
It is their name all day in the long light.
          *

We had long left the land of the honeybee.
Not since the Osage, but flowers sweet in season proper,
And the bee-martin comes. This we could not understand.
There was much not easy to understand, the mountains
To the right hand, the north, and west of us,
Boomed like a bell,
One great stroke lonely, or then more, and rapid
Like discharge of ordnance,
Six-pounders, the battery well-timed.
The Minnetarees had told us of it. We thought they lied.
But we who have heard the sound
Pretend to no understanding.

It is for philosophy to say. We were soldiers,
And simple. But recorded all days,
The little and large.
As when we slew a wolf: *This day a yellow wolf was slain.*
The winter broke: *The sugar maple runs freely;*
Swans pass from the north.
May came again: *The geese have their young, the elk begin*
To produce their young. The antelope and deer
As yet have not, the small species
Of whippoorwill begins to cry. We have scarce any thunder.
The clouds are generally white and accompanied
With wind only.

We moved across the land. We endured.
And after endurance the snarl of mutiny. I flogged him.
He screamed at the dawn-stripes. The Indians, watching, wept.
And I would have wept in my heart, for I knew him,
And knew him to be only another of us,
In long travel.

And we suffered the rigor of seasons,
White dew and sun-heat, and the time
When hibernants are withdrawn to the only comfort
In the iron world. And snow on the far peak glared blue
In excess of light, and no track of beast on the unruffled
White of the high plain, no wing-flash in high air,
And in that glittering silence of the continent
I heard my heart beating distinctly, and I said,

Is this delight? Is this the name of delight?

But tumors on legs, boils, impostumes. Some spat blood.
And disease of foulness from clipping the female savage.
The savages make a brew of lobelia and sumac, the roots.
We tried it to soften the *lues*. Of use, but not sovereign.
We saw and described new beasts. We slew the great bear,
The horrible one, gray-grizzle and does not forgive.
Men see his track on the sand bar and are afraid.
We noted his color and how his testicles are great, and hang
Uniquely under the belly.

The heart is of great size and death comes most tardy,
With anger. We ate
The flesh of dog, but rejoiced. We ate peculiar flesh.

I sat on the blanket with chiefs.
On white elk-hide Twisted Hair drew me a map,
How the rivers converged west and sought the great lake
Of water ill-tasted. Their name for the ocean. But none
Had been there. We came.
We lay on our mats in the rain. Heard the booming of ocean.

Next day we saw.
And Clark, my friend, wrote in his papers thus:
O Ocian in view! O! the joy.

And pride in endurance is one thing that shall not
Be denied men.

O! the joy, Clark cried, but the inwardness of that joy
Of our long travel together was not yet revealed.
To be revealed upon our return
When the faces of my companions
Were withdrawn from my sight,
And only imagination
Could speak truth of our common experience.

Truth? No: the last delusion. But that later.
                *

Now was November. We wintered by that water,
And heard the great boom steady when storm strode.
A long way back,
And returning we passed all the seasons.

Then St. Louis, and I broke bread with civil men.
Well, I had seen
The savage tear the steaming guts,
And blood streak the cheekbone,
And would that I had wallowed and remained there!

You had lied with persuasion to the need of my heart.
And for one brief moment my experience
Seemed confirmation of all you had said, for in
My imagination the voice remained of the night ocean,
And I thought that I knew
How men may long travel together, as brothers.

So Governor of Louisiana, of all the West,
Headquarters St. Louis—
But the small lies gathered,
Like midges over the mud-flats in the month of fever.
That Bates, whose hell-heart is a bog of ordure—
That Bates, he smiled. He stank in sunshine.

And so I fled.

Not westward as I should, but east,
And took my papers for my proof.
In Federal City, where you had sat,
There I'd find Justice—
Not guessing who the Great Betrayer was!

To Tennessee I came, at Chickasaw.
Drunk at Fort Pickering, not my custom.
I could not understand my own drunkenness.
Then in the wilderness found the Natchez Trace,
And fled. Fled my companions,
Fled their voices—
My Creole, my black boy, good Major Neeley.

I fled the human face and smile, and rode.
I rode toward Justice. I would kill the slander
That I—I who had slept under the big stars—
Would peck at dollars as a sparrow at dung.

To the miserable inn, at evening, I came.
Grinder's the name. A work-sick woman, brats.
The husband away. Two huts in the wilderness.
The desperate corn patch snagged with fire-black trees.

I asked for drink and took it, but not much.
I ate the food she gave me, but not much.
I could not understand my own agitation.
I sat outside the door and watched the evening.
"It is a beautiful evening," I said to the woman.
I thought, that moment, of the beauty of evening
Moving west over the infinite land.

Now in my cabin the woman spread my robes,
Bearskin and buffalo. I laid me down.
But not to sleep.
I rose alone and spoke aloud and declared myself.
In the disturbed darkness I declared myself.
For suddenly I knew there was no Justice.
For the human heart will hate Justice for its humanness.

Had I not dreamed that Man at last is Man's friend
And they will long travel together
And rejoice in steadfastness.
Had I not loved, and lived, your lie, then I
Had not been sent unbuckled and unbraced—
Oh, the wilderness was easy!—
But to find, in the end, the tracklessness
Of the human heart.

So seized the weapon primed and charged, and broke
In one blast the brain-pan, and flung the lie
To wing away, and let me sleep.

But could not die. Cried out for water.

Crawled in the moonlight, groped the gourd in the bucket.
But the bucket was empty, and nobody came.
Cried out: "I am no coward,
No coward, but so strong and hard to die!"
I remembered then how the great bear had died,
Tardy, with anger, under the plum trees. I knew him.

At dawn, I died.

I knew who murdered me.

I knew who flung my body in the hole
Where hog might root, or wolf scrabble.
And after the turn of years some pedant fool
Had chopped his Latin for my garnishment
And chiseled up the lie I'd never have spoke.
I'd never say: "Oh, Good Republic, live!
And happier live my lost years in your own."
Oh, no. That Good Republic is of men,
So let them live their own years and not mine.
I solemnly curse them,
The lies they live and the deeds of their hands,
And if you murdered me—

JEFFERSON: No, no, my son!

LILBURNE: Oh, it's dark, bring me a light!

LUCY: Brother, I begin to see—

JEFFERSON: I see what I see. The foul one.

LUCY: Oh, take Lil's hand in his darkness.

JEFFERSON: Which chopped the nigger to defend your spoons!

LUCY: Can you conceive
The soft-foot nightmare of that thought?

But no!—what he would have defended

Was but himself against the darkness that was his.
He felt the dark creep in from all the woods.
He felt the dark fear hiding in his heart.
He saw the dark hand set the white dish down.
He saw poor John as but his darkest self
And all the possibility of dark he feared.
And all he wanted—

JEFFERSON: Was blood.
I'll take no responsibility for that!

LUCY: I must accept the responsibility of my love.
Even though that love was infected by failure.
Even if I tried to flee responsibility, and
Died. Oh, don't repeat my crime.
Just take his hand.

MERIWETHER: Yes, take it! For, yes, I'd honor more
The axe in the midnight meat-house, as more honest at least,
Than your murderous lie to prove yourself
Nobler in man's nobleness.

JEFFERSON: Look—blood's slick on that hand!
You'd have me compound the crime?

LUCY: But you do compound it! By refusal.
For what poor Lilburne did in madness and exaltation,
You do it in vanity.

MERIWETHER: No—in fear.

JEFFERSON: I feared no man!

LUCY: Yes—yes—he's right—in fear!

JEFFERSON: Fear who?

LUCY: His name is Jefferson.

MERIWETHER: That's right, Old Jeff!
*

LUCY: Yes—and your deepest fear.
When you had learned in that report from Kentucky
What was possible even in the familial blood,
Then your fear began—

MERIWETHER: —that you were human. Human, too, Old Fellow!

LUCY: Your fear began, and in virtue and sick vanity
You'd strike poor Lilburne down—and—

MERIWETHER: Look at your arm—it's lifted! Is the axe there?
Ah, the rage of virtue! At your sister now.
Will you strike her down?

JEFFERSON: My son, be still a moment.
If what you call my lie undid you,
It has undone me too. For I, too,
Was unprepared for the nature of the world,
And I confess, for my own nature.
And Truth, long since, began her hideous justice.
But if there was vanity, if there—

LUCY: Dear Brother, the burden of innocence is heavier
Than the burden of guilt. If you
Loved innocence, then you must
Take his hand.

JEFFERSON: I see my hand. It hangs in the air.
I see it. Was it to strike?

MERIWETHER: And the fire flares red on your face
Where the sweat is! Think of sweat
Beading Lilburne's brow.

JEFFERSON: If I believe you, what is left for me?

LUCY: All's left that's worth the having.

JEFFERSON: If all I dreamed was but the reflex of—
Of what? Of vanity? Of—
                    *

LUCY: Your dream, dear Brother, was noble.
If there was vanity, fear, or deceit in its condition,
What of that? For we are human, and must work
In the shade of the human condition.

MERIWETHER: The dream remains?
I see it—yes. But see
A nobler yet to dream!

LUCY: It will be nobler because more difficult
And cold, in the face of the old cost
Of our complicities. And—

MERIWETHER: —knowledge of that cost is,
In itself, a kind of redemption.

JEFFERSON: I think I know what you would say to me.
One day I wrote to Adams, in our age—so long ago—
To Adams my old enemy and friend, that gnarled greatness.

I wrote and said
That the dream of the future is better than
The dream of the past.

How could I hope to find courage to say
That without the fact of the past, no matter
How terrible, we cannot dream the future?

MERIWETHER: I think I glimpse
The forging of the future—

JEFFERSON: Forged beneath the hammer of truth
On the anvil of our anguish!

LUCY: How terrible to think that truth may be lost.
But worse to think that anguish is lost, ever.

JOHN: I was lost in the world, and the trees were tall.
I was lost in the world and the dark swale heaved.
I was lost in my anguish and did not know the reason.
            *

JEFFERSON: Reason? That's the word
I sought to live by—but, oh,
We have been lost in the dark, and I
Was lost who had dreamed there was a light.
How could I show you now the light of reason
When I had lost it when your blood ran out?

But can it—can it be that we are condemned
To search for it?—
Oh, I'm a fool.

LUCY: No, Brother, touch him. Touch Lilburne.

JOHN: Yes—now is the time!—That's all I,
In my ignorance, know.

LUCY: He should know most.

JOHN: Oh, please!

JEFFERSON: Touch him—touch him—yes?

Yes, look! I've touched. Oh, may we hope to find—
No, thus create—

LUCY: —the possibility of reason. Yes,
And create it only from
Our most evil despair?

JEFFERSON: Yes, what steel striking
What stone may provoke,
In the midst of our coiling darkness,
The incandescence of the heart's great flare?

MERIWETHER: Dance back the buffalo, the Shining Land!
Our grander Ghost Dance dance now, and shake the feather.
Dance back the whole wide gleaming West anew!

ALL (singing):
Dance back the morning and the eagle's cry.

119

Dance back the Shining Mountains, let them shine!
Dance into morning and the lifted eye.
Dance into morning past the morning star,
And dance the heart by which we must live and die.

JEFFERSON: My Louisiana, I would dance you, though afar!

MERIWETHER: For nothing we had,
Nothing we were,
Is lost. All is redeemed,
In knowledge.

JEFFERSON: But knowledge is the most powerful cost.
It is the bitter bread.
I have eaten the bitter bread.
In joy, would end.

VI

R.P.W.: Consider those who could not end in joy.
Take John all huddled for the senseless axe,
Or old Aunt Cat, who lived too long. Or Letitia,
Who could never know what her own story meant.
Take Lilburne counting slow.
Take Isham—accessory they named, and the jury
Called for rope.

The day drew on, and appetite, no doubt,
Declined, as dawn broke fair to make the holiday,
But sport was lacking—sing, or drink, or fight,
But ne'er a rope to stretch. *Aw hell, git home!*

For Isham's up and gone.

Far off, in Frankfort, in the Capitol,
Old Governor Shelby dipped his quill
And wrote: *Five hundred dollars gold,*
For Isham, quick or dead. That ought to fetch him.
But Isham ne'er stayed jailed to mope and tarry.
He's made his tracks, him having a prejudice
Against all hemp and hanging and bad dreams.
So busted jail—

ISHAM: No, I ne'er busted jail.
Just laid in jail a-feared they'd hang me.
Ashamed of being scared, and knowing, too,
They ought to hang me, for I killed my brother.
But Old Tom Terry—he guarded jail and me—
One night he came and said, real soft:
"Was you to hit me now and leave me lay,
You might git off. You'll find a hoss all saddled,
Down in the willow thicket. Hit's my hoss."
"You mean?" I said. And him: "Lak ever-body knows,
You warn't what brung the meanness on."

But then I yelled: "But my brother, I killed him!"
He laughed, and said: "I seen 'em hang.
You wouldn't lak it, son." And I just stared.

"I'm gittin old," he laughed. "Don't hit me hard."

R.P.W.: And rode away, and never tarried.

ISHAM: Yeah, rode away, and threw my name away.
I wasn't nothing, not nobody now.
I said: "I'm nothing, nothing ever happened."

And rode, but knew the one durn thing
A man can't do is throw himself away.
So everything was there, I rode with *me*,
And in the dark I'd say: "Oh, Lord, I'm *me*!"
And then New Orleans—

R.P.W.: So that is true—the tale the riflemen
Brought back to tell the homefolks when
They'd finished that big turkey-shoot
With Andy Jackson at the cotton bales?
Oh, not like any turkey-shoot back home
At forty paces, and the turkey's head
Is not a barn door when it bobs up quick
From behind the log, and then, for the scattered corn,
Is down again. And that split second
Is your only chance.

ISHAM: No, Louisiana, and any fool could get his turkey.
With every turkey six feet tall
And gobbling slow and footing on the green,
With drums a-gobbling, too, to set the time,
And nary a log to duck their head behind.
And we was snugged behind nice cotton bales.

Durn fools, durn fools—to see 'em march so pretty,
With red clothes shining like a wedding was,
Just marching at you like they never cared
Your aim was true to leave 'em lay.

122

And that's what made you mad,
To be so brave like all you did was naught,
And dying nothing, they'd spit on it, and you.
It made you mad because you knew down deep
How scared you'd be if you was marching there.
So lay your aim, and take that fool, reload your Betsy.
Just take it easy, count your powder right.

Then we were yelling at the cotton bales.
And music playing "Hail, Columbia."
I jumped up high and yelled for glory,
But yelling, too, because they marched so pretty
Who came across the waters, far away,
To march so pretty till the slug bit home.
And yelling, too, for something deep inside me,
Like I was me again, with folks a minute.

Then it hit me.

Some durn red-coated fool out yonder,
Some durn last fool, his kind all dead around him,
Takes time to load and shoot
Just one more time, back at those bales.
'Twas me he found.

A rifle-plug like ours, it's small and true.
It goes in easy, not much blood comes out.
But muskets, hell—if you can hit a thing
It knocks a hole, goes *chunk*—it's messy.

It made a mess of me.

Somebody held my head to give me water.
He looked, and stared. He said: "Be durn!"

He knew me, Isham, and they knew my name,
Folks from back home, come here to kill some red-coats.
I died right easy while they named my name.

Like they forgave me—even if I killed my brother.
      *

R.P.W.: And now in the Smithland courthouse on the indictment
The Commonwealth as Plaintiff had drawn for murder,
We find endorsed:

> *The same Plaintiff*
> *against*
> *Isham Lewis Defendant*
> *Ordered that this suit be abated by*
> *The death of the defendant.*

That is all.
It is abated. All is abated now.

It is abated, and your brother now
Sleeps in his dusty triumph, all alone.
No, not alone, his mother sleeping nigh.
But there is no communication between them.
No tread intrudes on the common silence
And the jay's call is the index of indifference.
The ferocious tangle of blackberry
Is sovereign on the spot.

Nobody comes.

AUNT CAT: But me. Long time ago,
Afore the Lawd, He let me die,
When the world done tromped the sweetness out my heart.
Oh, Lil, oh, Chile, I come and seen and said:
"Whar is my Lil? He ain't beneath this ground.
Oh, ain't my Lil what puked my milk away!
Not Lil, oh, no—hit's some mean stranger, sly
To come and steal yore name and face away
And blame on Lil how Time and the world is awful,
And weevil in the meal, and spring run dry,
And folks don't love nobody—hit ain't my Lil."

Fer then I knowed whar my Lil come to stay.
My Lil, he come inside my heart to stay
And hang his hat and take his ease, and all
My heart gits singing and the fire dance bright.
Sings "Lil!" Sings "Lil! my leetle Baby-Bear."

124

Sings "Lil, won't nuthen git you now.
Raw-Head, Raw-Head, doan come my baby nigh.
Chile safe in Mammy's heart and shet the door.
Let Ole Wind blow, and let Ole Time blow by."

Chile safe asleep. I knowed the place he'll stay.

VII

R.P.W.: The actual body of Lilburne, or what remains,
Lies sixty paces, more or less, beyond
The ruin of the Lewis house, about northwest.
At last I went again.
It was December then. We left for Smithland,
And under the paleness of the lemon light,
The heart of the earth drew inward, and was still,
And a voice speaking, or a dog's bark,
Carried with calm and frosted ceremony
In sad perfection past the field and farm,

Tonight the heel will ring on the earth, like iron.

Now under the lemon light we move,
My father and I,
Across the landscape of his early experience.
We pass the land where stood the house of his first light.
No remnant remains of stone gone fire-black. The plow-point
Has passed where the sill lay.

The old house, square, set on limestone, by cedars
That I, in my mind, see,
Is not a house I have seen. It is
A fiction of human possibility past.
We whirl past the spot it held, now woods.
The grave of my father's father is lost in the woods.
The oak-root has heaved down the headstone.

My father says: "About this time, December,
I recollect my father, how he'd take
Some yellow percoon, the root, and mash it
And bark of prickly ash, and do the same,
And cram it in a gallon jug, with whiskey."

"What for?" I asked. "A drink?"
        *

"No, medicine, to wait three months on the shelf.
And spring came on, and then he'd call us boys—
All boys—we were a house of boys he had—
And line us up and give it, morn and night."

"What for?" I said.

"It's old-folks talk, but then they held it true,
My father said how winter thicked boys' blood
And made 'em fit for devilment, and mean.
But he'd sure fix that. Percoon would wry your tongue."

"But what's percoon?" And he: "Why, Son,
I just don't recollect. But it's percoon."

And so we passed that land and the weight of its mystery.
We passed the mystery of years and their logic,
And I have been a stranger in many nations.
I have been a stranger in my bed at night,
And with a stranger.
I have been a stranger when the waiter turned for my order.
I have been a stranger at the breaking of bread.
For isolation is the common lot
Which makes all mankind one.

And there was Smithland.
No, not Sam Clemens' town now, after all.
Sure, there's the jail, courthouse, and river,
And even now it's no metropolis,
In spite of a traffic signal, red and green,
And paint on houses, and new stores,
And money jingling in the local jeans.

Who would begrudge such solvency?
And who's to blame if there's a correlation
Between it and the dark audit of blood
In some Korean bunker, at the midnight concussion?
Yes, who's to blame? For in the great bookkeeping
Of History, what ledger has balanced yet?

                    *

In any case, Mr. Boyle's not home today—
Down in Paducah, I guess, for Christmas shopping.
But white, with new paint, the house shines in the sun.

I enter the barn lot. I see the new difference.
The barn's been propped, and in the bright
Cold sun the cattle stand. Some twenty head,
And whiteface, too. The jaws
Move slow. The bright drool drips in sun,
And under the glossy flanks the full flesh bulges
With the deep delight of being flesh, for flesh
Is its own blessing, and nobility.

Why am I here? But there's the bluff. I'd better climb.

Strange now, today it doesn't look so high,
Not like it did the first time here.
July it was—and I damned the heat and briar,
Then clambered through the tall, hot gloom
Of oak and ironwood, where grapevine, big as boas,
Had shagged and looped
In jungle convolvement and visceral delight.
For that's the way I had remembered it.

But, no, it's not quite that. At least, not now,
And never was, perhaps, but in my head.
There's grapevine, sure, and big,
But hanging like it's tired
From trees gone leafless now, and not so tall.
So I'm prepared for what I find up yonder:
The ruin now shrunken to a heap,
And those fine beech trees that I'd celebrated,
They just aren't there at all, or two or three,
Just piddling shag-barks, walnuts two or three,
And oaks to middling, not to brag on.

So winter makes things small, all things draw in.

I had plain misremembered,
Or dreamed a world appropriate for the tale.

One thing, however, true: old *obsoleta*
Had reared that day, and swayed against the sun.
But not today. He's keeping home this weather,
Down in the rocks, I reckon, looped and snug
And dark as dark: in dark the white belly glows,
And deep behind the hog-snout, in that blunt head,
The ganglia glow with what cold dream is congenial
To fat old *obsoleta*, winterlong.

All things draw inward with the winter's will.
The snow lies thin and pure, and I lift my eyes
Beyond the bluff and flatlands farther
Where the river gleams.
Its gleam is cold.

And I think of another bluff and another river.
I think of snow on brown leaves, and below
How cold and far was light on a northern river,
And think how her mouth and mine together
Were cold on the first kiss. We kissed in the cold
Logic of hope and need.

Who is to name delusion when the flesh shakes?

So in this other year by another river,
Far in Kentucky there, I raised my eyes
And thought of the track a man may make through Time,
And how the hither-coming never knows the hence-going.
Since then I have made new acquaintance
With snow on brown leaves.
Since then I have made new acquaintance
With the nature of joy.

I stood on the bluff and thought how men
Had moved on that broad flood—the good, the bad,
The strong, the weak, the drawn, the driven,
The fortunate, the feckless, all men, a flood
Upon the flood, and I,
In that cold light, was impelled to apostrophize:

River, who have on your broad bosom borne
Man and man's movement, and endured the oar,
Keel-pole and paddle, sweep and paddle-wheel.
And suffered the disturbance of the screw's bronze blade,
And tissued over that perpetual scarification
With instant sweetness and confident flow—
You who have suffered filth and the waste
Of the human establishment,
Ordure of Louisville and the slick of oil,
The drowned cow, swollen, from the mountain cove,
And junk jammed on the sand bar in the sun—
I take you as an image
Of that deep flood that is our history,
And the flood that makes each new day possible
And bears us westward to the new land.
I take you as image and confirmation
Of some faith past our consistent failure,
And the filth we strew.

And so I thought of the dead beneath my feet.
Of Lilburne on his mountain here,
Who brought no light into the dark, so died.
And of another mountain, far away,
In Albemarle, where Lilburne's kinsman sleeps,
And thought of all
Who had come down the great river and are
Nameless. What if
We know the names of the niggers hunkering by the wall,
Moaning? For yes, we know each name,
The age, the sex, the price, from the executor,
Who listed all to satisfy the court.

And know the names of all who went with Meriwether
To lie on night-mats in rain, and hear the utterance of ocean.

We know that much, but what is knowledge
Without the intrinsic mediation of the heart?

Returned to St. Louis. Were mustered out. Took pay,
And stepped into the encroachment of shadow.

So years go by, but on some village bench,
Or in some grog-shop where the candle stutters
On shadowy foulness of fat fumes,
The gaffer leans, befogged by drink or age,
And strikes his knee, or table top,

And says: "God-durn, I seen it, I was thar!"
And they: "Hell, Pap, shet up, you're drunk again."

Yes, Pap, you saw it. We believe you, Pap.
For we were there, too, and saw it, and heard
The mountain, like a bell,
Lonely, boom, though no geologist admits it possible.
We have seen the great bear die.
We have lifted the meat-axe in the elation of love and justice.
We have seen a small boy, wide-eyed, stand on the hearthstone
And accept from his father's hand
The bitter dose of percoon.

We have yearned in the heart for some identification
With the glory of the human effort. We have devised
Evil in the heart, and pondered the nature of virtue.
We have stumbled into the act of justice, and caught,
Only from the tail of the eye, the flicker
Of joy, like a wing-flash in thicket.

And so I stood on the headland and stared at the river
In the last light of December's, and the day's, declension.
I thought of the many dead and the places where they lay.
I looked at the shrunken ruin, and the trees leafless.
The winter makes things small. All things draw in.

It is strange how that shift of scale may excite the heart.

I leaned above the ruin and in my hand picked up
Some two or three pig-nuts, with the husks yet on.
I put them in my pocket. I went down.

Perhaps never to come back, for I did not know
What here remained, at least for me;

And to this day have not gone back, but hold,
In my heart, that landscape.

I crossed the evening barnlot, opened
The sagging gate, and was prepared
To go into the world of action and liability.
I had long lived in the world of action and liability.
But now I passed the gate into a world

Sweeter than hope in that confirmation of late light.

NOTES

Page 28

In 1785 the commission appointed to superintend the construction of a capitol in Richmond, Virginia, appealed to Jefferson for advice. He describes, in his autobiography, his response to this request:

> Thinking it a favorable opportunity of introducing into the State an example of architecture in the classic style of antiquity, and the Maison Quarrée of Nismes, an ancient Roman temple, being considered as the most perfect model existing of what may be called Cubic architecture, I applied to M. Clerisseau, who had published drawings of the Antiquities of Nismes, to have me a model of the building made in stucco, only changing the order from Corinthian to Ionic, on account of the difficulty of the Corinthian capitals . . . To adapt the exterior to our use, I drew a plan for the interior, with the apartments necessary for legislative, executive, and judiciary purposes; and accommodated in their size and distribution to the form and dimensions of the building. These were forwarded to the directors in 1786, and were carried into execution.

It was not until the next year—in March of 1787—that Jefferson saw the actual building at Nîmes. In a letter to the Comtesse de Tesse, a cousin of Lafayette, Jefferson delineates, somewhat whimsically, his grand architectural passion:

> Here I am, Madam, gazing whole hours at the Maison Quarrée, like a lover at his mistress. The stocking weavers and silk spinners around it consider me a hypochondriac Englishman about to write with a pistol the last chapter of his history. This is the second time I have been in love since I left Paris. The first was with a Diana at the Chateau de Laye-Epinaye in Beaujolais, a delicious morsel of sculpture by M. A. Slodtz. This, you will say, was in rule, to fall in love with a female beauty; but with a house! it is out of all precedent.

Page 64

The passage on the *annus mirabilis* is drawn from the following letter:

> Many things conspired to make the year 1811 the *annus mirabilis* of the West. During the earlier months, the waters of many of the great rivers overflowed their banks to a vast extent, and the whole country was in many parts covered from bluff to bluff. Unprecedented sickness followed. A spirit of change and recklessness seemed to pervade the very inhabitants of the forest. A countless multitude of squirrels, obeying some great and universal impulse, which none can know but the Spirit that gave them being, left their reckless and gambolling life and their ancient places of retreat in the North, and were seen pressing forward by tens of thousands in a deep and solid phalanx to the South. No obstacles seemed to check their extraordinary and concerted movement. The word had been given them to go forth, and they obeyed it, though multitudes perished in the broad Ohio, which lay in their path. The splendid comet of that year long continued to shed its twilight over the forests, and as autumn drew to a close, the whole valley of the Mississippi, from the Missouri to the Gulf, was shaken to its centre by continued earthquakes.

C. J. Latrobe, The Rambler in North America
Vol. 1 (New York, 1835)

I am indebted to Miss Eudora Welty for calling my attention to this account.

Pages 85–86

We the subscribers being called by the Coroner of this County of Livingston and St of Ky to hold an inquest on the Dead body of Jimmy a Chicisaw Indian in the house of James Levy in this town of Eddyville having examined the body of the said Jimmy do find the said Jimmy received several wounds in his head some of which appeared to have been made by strokes of a Club or Clubs in one place on his head the Scull seemed indented one wound in his head was about five inches long another about three inches long at right angles from the other those were apparently made by two or more strokes beside which we found one considerable burned spot on his back his nose was badly hurt we find the deceased was badly kicked about his face by means of all which wounds the said Indian has lost his life and that the wounds were given by Ruben Cook and Isaac Ferguson who are now in Gaol in this Town

Page 99

March 19, 1812

The grand jury returned sev presentments and disch^d.

Lilburn Lewis appeared in court in discharge of his recognizance and the grand having found an indictment against him and Isham Lewis for murder and the said Isham L. being in court they were ordered into the custody of the sheriff Whereupon the Defendants by their council moved the court to hear the evidence upon an application to admit the prisoners to bail Tomorrow morning at 9 o'clock and upon the application of the defendants to recognize the witnesses to appear on Tomorrow. Lilburn Lewis, Archibald Cannon, William Dyer Ackn^d themselves indebted in $200 each conditioned to appear here tomorrow
    Ordered that Court adjourned to tomorrow 9 o'clock

Page 103

In the name of God Amen This my last Will Ac. 1st It my desire that all my Just debts be paid and then my property both real and personal be equally divided between my children Jane W Lewis, Lucy I Lewis, Lilburn L Lewis, Elizabeth Lewis, Robert Lewis and James R Lewis reserving to my beloved but cruel wife Latitia G. Lewis her Lawful part of said property during her natural life. 2nd It my desire that my beloved father Charles L Lewis be possessed of the riding horse which I purchased of Hurley my rifle and shot bag during his natural life also my walking cane and that my beloved sisters Martha C Lewis Lucy B Lewis and Nancy M Lewis may be comforted from the perquisites of s^d estate by my executors as providence may require or in other words so as to do my children and themselves entire Justice. 3rd I do hereby constitute my beloved father Charles L Lewis the rev^d Wm Woods near Salem Saml C Harknes James MCawley and Arch^d Ferguson my executors whoom I must remind that Huey F. Delaney has received a fee from me for the prosecution in a Trespass against James Rutter sen^r, James Rutter Jr James Young and Thomas Terry given under my hand this and revoking all and every other will heretofore made, nineth day of Apr^l. Eighten hundred and Twelve Lilburn Lewis

NB. My dog Nero I do hereby bequeath to my beloved father L.D.

Rocky Hill Aprl 9th 1812. Mr. James MCawley I have fallen a victim to my beloved but cruel Letitia I die in the hope of being united to my other wife in heaven take care of this will and come here that we may be decently buried Adew—L. Lewis

NB. Within this inclosure myself and brother requests be entered in the same coffin and in the same ground grave

Rocky Hill Apr 10th 1812 my beloved but cruel Letitia receive this as a pledge of my forgiveness to your connections the day of Judgment is to come I owe you no malice but die on account of your Absence and my dear little son James Adieu my love

Lilburn Lewis

Livingston County SLC May County Court 1812 The within will was proven to be the handwriting of Lilburn Lewis by William Rice James MCawley and Lilburn Lewis sen^r and ordered to be recorded

Test Enoch Prince

We of the Jury are of the opinion that Lilburn Lewis Did murder
him self on the 10ᵗʰ Day of April 1812 on his own plantation and
acessary
Isham Lewis ~~first~~ present and ~~axeesary~~ to the Murder

Wᵐ Rutter fore Mⁿ.

Jury   upon oath
Isham Lewis before the   and saith that him self and Lilbourne Lewis
agreed to present a gun at each others breast and fire at a word with an
intention of killing each other—but that Lilbourne in in trying an experiment accidentally shot him self dead

April 11ᵗʰ 1812

Sworn to
before ——————————————————— John Darrah
Coroner L C

The details of the Lewis and Clark expedition are drawn from their
journals, especially the entries for the following dates:
1804: February 11 and October 14.
1805: January 5, April 29, May 5, May 11, May 17, June 10, July 2,
     July 4, August 16, August 20, September 22, November 7.
1806: January 21.
    The entry of July 4, 1805, discusses the great sound heard in the
mountains. The members of the expedition heard it on various occasions,
the single bell-like stroke or the succession of sounds like the discharge
of a battery of six-pounders at a distance of about three miles. The
same phenomenon had been reported by the Pawnees and Ricaras in
the Black Mountains, and I have read an account of such a sound in the
mountains of Arkansas, given by Thomas Nuttall, a trained scientist,
who published *A Journal of Travels into the Arkansas Territory during
the Year 1819* (Philadelphia, 1881). An eminent geologist whom I have
questioned informs me that science has no explanation of this phenome-

non, and he himself is strongly inclined to doubt the veracity of the record. The explanation given Lewis and Clark by their French watermen was that the sound came from the bursting of rich lodes of silver confined in the bosom of the mountains.

Page 115

Meriwether Lewis died in what is now Lewis County, Tennessee, some seventy-five miles southwest of Nashville. His monument is a broken plinth, erected by the Legislature of Tennessee, in 1848. The inscriptions are as follows:

(West face)

Meriwether Lewis
Born near Charlottesville, Virginia, August 18, 1774
Died October 11, 1809, aged 35 years

(South face)

An officer of the Regular Army—Commander of the Expedition
to the Oregon in 1803–1806—Governor of the Territory
of Louisiana—His melancholy death occurred
where this monument now stands, and
under which rest his mortal
remains.

(East face)

In the language of Mr. Jefferson: "His courage was undaunted;
his firmness and perseverance yielded to nothing but im-
possibilities; A rigid disciplinarian, yet tender
as a father of those committed to his charge;
honest, disinterested, liberal, with
a sound understanding and a
scrupulous fidelity
to truth."

(North face)

Immaturus obi; sed tu felicior annos
Vive meos, Bona Respublica! Vive tuos.

138

From the time of the eighteenth century, when the white settlers first broke in force across the mountains, there had been occasional bursts of excitement among the Indians at the notion of a Messiah who would restore their old life. But after the Civil War, when the Indians of the West were in the last paroxysm of resistance and despair, the religion of the Ghost Dance appeared. The founder—Jack Wilson to the whites and Wovoka to the Indians—was a Paiute Indian, son of Tavibo the prophet, born in Mason Valley, Nevada.

Wovoka was a dreamer and mystic who gave a dance to his people, and who on one occasion, at the time of a total eclipse of the sun, went into a trance and was taken to the other world, where he saw God and all the beloved dead, who were happy at their old sports and occupations in a land teeming with buffalo and elk. God told Wovoka that he must return and preach a gospel of love and peace, of industriousness and truth, and that if the Indians followed the gospel, they would in the end enter into the blessed world. In Wovoka's own words: "When the sun died I went up to heaven and saw God and all the people who had died a long time ago. God told me to come back and tell my people they must be good and love one another, and not fight, or steal, or lie. He gave me this dance to give to my people."

The news of the promise swept over the West, and assumed many forms. There was, for instance, the notion among the Cheyenne, Arapaho, and other tribes that the new shining earth would come sliding from the West over the old worn-out earth, and that the living Indians would be lifted up and transported to it by the aid of the sacred dance feathers in their hair which would serve as wings. Some held that there would be a wall of fire before the New Earth to drive the whites away, and some held that there would be a great cataclysmic shaking of the old earth, perhaps accompanied by a flood from which only the Indians would be saved to live in the shining land among the happy resurrected dead and the fat heads of buffalo. The Sioux, of course, did not wait for that moment, but took matters into their own hands with the outbreak of 1890.

As for the dance itself, it was circular, with a slow, dragging step, accompanied by song, interrupted now and then for exhortation or recitation by the medicine man. When a dancer began to show signs of the trance the medicine man would shake the eagle feather in front of the subject's eyes until the seizure had its full force and the dreamer fell down to enjoy his vision of the New Earth. Mothers sometimes brought toys or garments to give to dead children whom they might encounter in the trance.

For further information about the Ghost Dance, see *The Ghost-Dance Religion and the Sioux Outbreak of 1890*, by James Mooney, in the *Fourteenth Annual Report of the Bureau of Ethnology*, Part 2, and *The Pawnee Ghost Dance Hand Game*, by Alexander Lesser, New York, 1933.

Page 122

On January 8, 1815, on the plain of Chalmette, five miles out of New Orleans, General Pakenham, brother-in-law of Wellington, led an army of toughened veterans of the Peninsula Campaign against Andrew Jackson's rag-tag-and-bobtail, improvised army of Tennessee militia, Tennessee and Kentucky frontier riflemen, and pirates, who were fortified, among other materials, by commandeered cotton bales, and supported by well-served artillery. Wave on wave of organized assault was slaughtered by marksmanship, and organized volley at short range. The English loss was 700 dead, 1,400 wounded, 500 prisoners. Toward the end of the engagement, the United States band struck up "Hail, Columbia." They had lost 8 dead.

The battle occurred two weeks after the Treaty of Ghent had been signed, the treaty that ended the War of 1812. It was a time of slow communication.

Page 124

Monday the 20th March 1815

The same Plaintiff
against
Isham Lewis   Defendant
Ordered that this suit abate by the
death of the defendant.*

* *On the back of the indictment for murder.*

January the 2nd 1813

Agreeable to an order of the Livingston County Court appointing us commissioners to appraise the negroes belonging to the estate of Lilburne Lewis dec^d and to allott Latetia G. Lewis widow of said Lilburne Lewis dec^d her third part of said negroes we met at the house of James Rutter sen^r on the day above mentioned and valued said negroes as follows Towit Ceolio one hundred and fifty dollars William one hundred and Ten dollars Mosley three hundred and Twenty five dollars Carter four hundred and thirty-five dollars Aggy three hundred and fifty dollars Isaac two hundred and seventy five dollars Patsy Two hundred and eighty five dollars Archie four hundred and seventy five dollars Mary two hundred and Twenty-five dollars we then proceeded to assign to the widow the following negroes Towit Ceolio William Frank an Usley [Mosley?] witness our hands this day and date above written

> John Mott
> S C Harknis   Comm^s
> Joseph Rice

ABOUT THE AUTHOR

ROBERT PENN WARREN was born in Guthrie, Kentucky, in 1905. After graduating summa cum laude from Vanderbilt University (1925), he received a master's degree from the University of California (1927), and did graduate work at Yale University (1927–28) and at Oxford as a Rhodes Scholar (B.Litt., 1930).

Mr. Warren has published many books, including ten novels, twelve volumes of poetry, a volume of short stories, a play, a collection of critical essays, a biography, two historical essays, and two studies of race relations in America. This body of work has been published in a period of forty-nine years—a period during which Mr. Warren has also had an active career as a professor of English.

All the King's Men (1946) was awarded the Pulitzer Prize for Fiction. The Shelley Memorial Award recognized Mr. Warren's early poetry. *Promises* (1957) won the Pulitzer Prize for Poetry, the Edna St. Vincent Millay Prize of the Poetry Society of America, and the National Book Award. In 1944–45 Mr. Warren was the second occupant of the Chair of Poetry at the Library of Congress. In 1952 he was elected to the American Philosophical Society; in 1959 to the American Academy of Arts and Letters; and in 1975 to the American Academy of Arts and Sciences. He is a Chancellor of the Academy of American Poets. In 1967 he received the Bollingen Prize in Poetry for *Selected Poems: New and Old, 1923–1966*, and in 1970 the National Medal for Literature and the Van Wyck Brooks Award for the book-length poem *Audubon: A Vision*. In 1974 he was chosen by the National Endowment for the Humanities to deliver the third Annual Jefferson Lecture in the Humanities. In 1975 he received the Emerson-Thoreau Award of the American Academy of Arts and Sciences. In 1976 he received the Copernicus Award from the Academy of American Poets, in recognition of his career but with special notice of *Or Else—Poem/ Poems 1968–1974*. In 1977 he received the Harriet Monroe Prize for Poetry. *Now and Then* (1978) received the Pulitzer Prize for Poetry.

Mr. Warren lives in Connecticut with his wife, Eleanor Clark (author of *Rome and a Villa*, *The Oysters of Locmariaquer*, *Baldur's Gate*, and *Eyes, Etc.: A Memoir*), and their two children, Rosanna and Gabriel.